Evangelism
for the
Fainthearted

Evangelism
for the
Fainthearted

FLOYD SCHNEIDER

kregel
PUBLICATIONS

Grand Rapids, MI 49501

Evangelism for the Fainthearted

© 1991, 2000 by Floyd E. Schneider
Second Edition

Published by Kregel Publications, a division of Kregel, Inc.,
P.O. Box 2607, Grand Rapids, MI 49501. Kregel Publications
provides trusted, biblical publications for Christian growth
and service. Your comments and suggestions are valued.

For more information about Kregel Publications, visit our
web site: www.kregel.com

Library of Congress Cataloging-in-Publication Data
Schneider, Floyd E.
    Evangelism for the fainthearted / by Floyd E. Schneider.—
Rev., updated ed.
        p.   cm.
    Includes bibliographical references.
    1. Witness bearing (Christianity). I. Title.
BV4520 S28   2000   269'.2–dc21   99-057654
                                               CIP

ISBN 0-8254-3795-4

Printed in the United States of America

1 2 3 4 5 / 04 03 02 01 00

To my in-house editor;
to a much better author than
the one who wrote this book;
to the most supportive wife a man could
ever dream of finding:
Christine

An excellent wife, who can find? For her worth is far
above jewels. . . . She does him good and not evil all the
days of her life. . . . Her children rise up and bless her;
Her husband also, and he praises her. . . . A woman who
fears the LORD, she shall be praised.
—Proverbs 31:10, 12, 28, 30

Special thanks to:
John Lennox—for inspiration
Roger and Karolyn—for technical assistance
Sharon Mathews—for sacrificial proofreading

Contents

Foreword

What could be more basic to evangelism than the Bible? Or more effective in leading people to faith in Jesus Christ than reading–simply reading–God's Word with them?

Why was the Bible written? To explain the complexities of human government? To critique certain theories of economics? To teach us the wonders of astronomy?

The primary purpose of the Bible is not to tell us how the heavens go, but how to go to heaven. The Bible's great message is that God desires to transform the lives of people through His Word, preparing them for eternity with Him in glory.

God's Word has power to transform individuals from condemned sinners to redeemed believers. I know this personally, because a British gentleman named Frank Chandler brought me to saving faith in Jesus Christ by reading Romans 10:9-10 to me.

I was only twelve years old when I sincerely committed my life to Christ through prayer, but from that moment on, I knew I was a child of God. I knew I was going to heaven when I died. Christ had paid for my sins by His death on the cross.

Conversion–the transformation of an individual from a sinner to a child of God–is impossible apart from God's Word. Missionaries brought God's saving Word to Argentina, where I grew up. Because of their work, my father and mother are in heaven. Millions of people around the world, including myself, thank God for the missionaries who brought God's Word.

The Bible has the power to transform anyone, anywhere–the high or low, the rich or poor, the educated or illiterate. I have seen the Word of God transform the lives of many, many people:

a former president of Bolivia . . . an illiterate janitor . . . a
princess in Britain . . . the prime minister of a South Pacific
nation . . . a movie star in El Salvador . . . an East Coast disk
jockey . . . a nightclub singer . . . punk rockers in Poland . . .
a banker's daughter, sixteen and pregnant out of wedlock . . .
mayors of several cities . . . gang members . . . spiritists . . .
couples in the process of filing for divorce . . . a military
general's wife . . . ambassadors . . . agnostics . . .
atheists . . . Hindus . . . Buddhists . . . Muslims . . . and a
good number of nominal "Christians."

Years ago, during a live call-in program I was doing in the
studios of HCJB in Quito, Ecuador, a high-pitched, squeaky voice
requested an appointment with me for the next day at 9:30. No
more conversation. When I agreed, the squeaky voice thanked
me and hung up.

The next morning, a little woman walked through the gates at
HCJB, followed closely by two huge men. As she entered the office, I asked if the two gentlemen would like to come in, too. "No,"
she said, "one will stand by the door and the other by the gate." It
was the squeaky voice from the night before. She was right on time.

She spoke with a sneer, and venom poured out of her. "You
pastors and priests," she began with disgust. "You are a bunch
of thieves and liars and crooks. All you want is to deceive people;
all you want is money!"

She went on that way for more than twenty minutes, swear-
ing constantly and accusing, criticizing, and insulting. I had no
idea how to react and couldn't have gotten a word in anyway. I
prayed silently, *Lord, how shall I handle this?*

Seemingly exhausted from the ordeal, she finally slumped in
her chair like a jogger who has just finished a tough course. She
took a deep breath, her eyes still flashing.

"Madam," I began, "is there anything I can do for you? How
can I help you?"

She slowly took her cigarette from her lips and sat staring at
me for an instant, then suddenly broke into uncontrollable sobs.
When she was composed and could speak again, the edge was

gone from her voice. "You know," she said, "in the thirty-eight years I have lived, you are the first person who has ever asked if he could help me."

"What is your name?" I asked.

She was suddenly hard again. "Why do you want to know my name?"

"Well, you've said a lot of things here, and I don't even know you. I just want to know how to address you."

She sat back in her chair and straightened up a bit. Cocking her head and looking at me out of the corner of her eye, she lifted her chin and took yet another drag at her cigarette. Then she said with finality, "I'm going to tell you," as if allowing me a real privilege.

"My name is Maria ——," she said triumphantly. I recognized her last name as that of a large family of wealth and influence. "I am the secretary of the Communist Party here in Ecuador. I am a Marxist-Leninist, and I am a materialist. I don't believe in God."

With that she took off on another breathless tirade against all preachers and priests, the church, the Bible, and anything else she could think of that rivaled her beliefs.

"Why did you come here?" I broke in. "Just to insult me?"

She was thoughtful again. "I'm going to tell you my story," she announced. And for the next three hours, without pause or interruption, she did just that.

She had been a rebellious teenager who ran away from a religious school and was given a choice by her parents: return to school or leave the family. She left. The communists befriended her and took her in. Within the next few years, she married and divorced three times and had several children.

Despite her upbringing, she became a party leader and organized student rebellions. She made it quite clear that, as a Marxist-Leninist, she opposed everything that Christianity stood for.

Three hours after she began, we finally got down to business.

"Listen, Palau," Maria said. "Supposing there is a God—and I'm not saying there is, because I don't believe in the Bible, and

I don't believe there's a God—but just supposing there is. Just for the sake of chatting about it, if there is a God, which there isn't, do you think He would receive a woman like me?"

The Lord gave me Hebrews 10:17, one of my favorite Bible verses because it is so short and says so much: "Their sins and their lawless deeds I will remember no more."

I said, "Look, Maria, don't worry about what I think; look at what God thinks." I opened to the verse and turned the Bible so she could see it.

"But I don't believe in the Bi—"

"You've already told me that," I said. "But we're just supposing there's a God, right? Let's just suppose this is His Word. He says, 'Their sins and their lawless deeds I will remember no more.'"

She waited, as if there had to be more. I said nothing. "But listen. I've been an adulteress, married three times, and in bed with a lot of different men."

I said, "'Their sins and their lawless deeds I will remember no more,'" and began to count the times I repeated it.

"But I haven't told you half my story. I stabbed a comrade who later committed suicide."

"'Their sins and their lawless deeds I will remember no more.'"

"I've led student riots where people were killed!"

"'Their sins and their lawless deeds I will remember no more.'"

"I egged on my friends and then hid while they were out dying for the cause."

"'Their sins and their lawless deeds I will remember no more.'"

Seventeen times I responded to Maria's objections and confessions with that one Bible verse. It was past lunchtime. I was tired and weak. I had no more to offer. "Would you like Christ to forgive all that you've told me about, and all the rest that I don't even know?"

She was quiet. Finally she spoke softly. "If He could forgive me and change me, it would be the greatest miracle in the world." I led her in a simple prayer of commitment. By the end, she was crying.

Maria returned a week later to tell me she was reading the

Bible. Eventually, despite death threats and a brutal beating by her comrades, she resigned from the Communist Party. In fact, her witness to party leaders and invitation to read the Bible thwarted plans for a student-led disturbance that was supposed to trigger a revolution.

"For the word of God is living and active and sharper than any two-edged sword, and piercing as far as the division of soul and spirit, of both joints and marrow, and able to judge the thoughts and intentions of the heart" (Heb. 4:12).

Floyd Schneider's simple but profound premise for this book is that Christians don't have to have all the answers to be effective in evangelism. The Bible has the answers. In the power of the Holy Spirit, all we need to do is ask people to read Scripture with us. Even the fainthearted—that includes most of us—can do that!

—Luis Palau
international evangelist and author of
Where Is God When Bad Things Happen? (Doubleday)

Chapter 1

The Fear

Overcoming Evangelism Jitters

"Have you ever thought about God?" Mark asked, as Anthony set his lunch tray on the table and took a seat opposite him.

Anthony's expression told Mark that it was going to be an unpleasant lunch hour. "You're not on a religious trip, are you?" Anthony sneered.

"No, I just wondered if you ever thought about God." The dining room was filling up quickly, and other people were sitting near them. Mark wished he hadn't asked the question.

"Why should I think about God?" Anthony retorted—louder than necessary, Mark thought. "When has He ever spared a thought about me?"

Two young women looked in their direction. Mark felt his face start to turn red. Why had he tried to witness to Anthony? He had known he would fail.

Anthony had picked up his fork but hadn't eaten anything yet. He was waiting in mocking expectancy for Mark's reply.

Mark swallowed and answered, "He died on the cross for your sins, for one thing."

The giggles and muffled laughter from the two women and two men at their table reached Mark's ears almost before he had finished his sentence.

Anthony took advantage of being in the majority. "That's a

joke! Jesus may have been a good man, but He was certainly misguided. Look where it got Him—a cross. His crazy disciples cooked up that story of His dying for sins so they could justify having followed Him."

Before Mark could respond, Anthony continued. "Mark, how can you believe in God? I'm really disappointed in you. I really didn't expect that you would throw out your logic for an old wives' tale. How can a thinking person believe in religion?"

Mark knew he was lost, but now his pride was wounded, so he said defensively, "I've read the Bible."

One of the young men at the other end of the table applauded loudly enough for everyone in the dining room to hear, "Bravo!"

Anthony shook his head and replied, "You don't take the Bible seriously, do you? The Bible is completely unscientific and out-of-date. The only people who use the Bible are either very naive or they use the Bible to prey on the ignorance and superstitions of others."

Mark opened his mouth to reply, but as he glanced around, he saw all eyes on him, as if the entire student body was waiting, breathlessly, for him to stick his foot into his mouth again. He could see sheer delight on a number of faces as they watched him squirm in his seat.

And then a bell rang, and the spell was broken. Anthony left without his usual "see you later," and many other people looked pointedly in Mark's direction and sniggered as they left the dining room.

Mark felt that his best option would be to change his identity and leave the country.

Have you ever had this kind of experience? If not, have you ever lived under the dread of something similar happening to you? Maybe you can visualize it: You bring up the subject of God or the Bible, your friend makes an objection that never occurred to you, and you stand there, feeling like a fool, not knowing what to say, wishing that someone had taught you how to make yourself disappear. Then you know you will only make things worse if you reply, so you say nothing and decide that you'll leave evangelism to the experts.

Many of us want to obey the Lord's Great Commission in Matthew 28:18–20, but we are afraid that our inept attempts to witness will simply drive our friends away. We feel frustrated and wonder why the Lord commanded all of us to share our faith but gave only some believers the gift of evangelism.

If you feel this way, then this book is written for you. (If you have the gift of evangelism, you probably should have bought a different book!) When the Lord told His disciples in Acts 1:8 that they would be His witnesses, He meant all of them, not just a few gifted believers. In 1 Peter 3:15, Peter tells us as believers to sanctify Christ as Lord in our hearts, always being ready to make a defense to everyone who asks us to give an account for the hope that is in us.

Believers have used many methods of evangelism over the centuries, and the Lord has blessed them mightily: outdoor tent meetings, door-to-door surveys, tract distribution, various evangelistic visitation programs, and city-wide campaigns carried out by churches working together to bring a well-known evangelist to their city.

Apart from times of great revivals, however, these methods have normally produced the best results only because they were coupled with personal contact between believers and their unsaved friends. Missionaries and believers from America, various European countries, and Israel, among others, have told me over the past few years that although they have tried various evangelistic methods in these modern, advanced countries, the only visible progress they have made in evangelism has been through personal friendship with the unsaved. These friendships then led to Bible studies or evangelistic meetings or campaigns.

Walter Martin wrote:

> More and more, Christians are beginning to think in terms of *personal* evangelism as opposed to mass evangelism, primarily because all *successful* evangelism of enduring worth, has been of a personal nature. . . . The follow-up work of every major evangelical crusade must

be on a personal basis to be effective. A stamped enve-
lope and a short memory course are no substitute for
the personal workers, whose on-the-spot faithfulness,
patience and perseverance builds up and edifies young
converts after the first warm glow of the conversion
experience has begun to abate. . . . Is it perhaps possible that evangelism was intended, in its primary purpose, to be personal and individualistic to the degree
that each Christian feels the responsibility to evangelize his neighbor, and that this is really the root of the
whole matter from which the tree of church evangelism
and mass evangelism, both in crusades and the mass
media, are to draw their strength and spiritual stamina?[1]

A person with whom you have become friends will usually be
far more receptive to attending an evangelistic meeting and listening to the gospel than will a person who does not know you
very well. A person with whom you have been reading the Bible
will be even more receptive to such an invitation.

In this book, I hope to do more than just prepare you to
invite an unsaved person to an evangelistic meeting. I want you
to experience the joy of actually leading one of your friends to
Christ. The method—if it can be called a method—with which
this book deals emphasizes reading the Bible with a friend. It is
not meant to be used as a spur-of-the-moment witnessing tool
by which the believer gives an unsaved person the whole gospel
in one short, five-minute shot. *Our goal is to make our friends
curious enough to read the Bible with us.* Time is required to
develop a personal relationship with an unsaved person. Reading the Bible with an unsaved friend is our ultimate objective.

Why read the Bible together, instead of simply telling our
friends the gospel? An example will best answer this question.

A few years ago, a Christian attended a university on the East
Coast of America and shared a room with a young man who
was a Muslim. During the first few weeks, they became friends,
and one night the conversation turned to their different beliefs.

After a couple of long conversations, the believer asked the Muslim if he had ever read the Bible. The young man answered no, but then he asked if the Christian had ever read the Koran.

The believer responded, "No, I haven't read the Koran, but I'm sure it would be very interesting. Why don't we read both together, once a week, alternating books?"

The young man accepted the challenge, and their friendship deepened over the weeks. During the second term, the Muslim became a believer in Jesus Christ.

One evening, toward the end of the second term, he burst into the room and shouted at the believer, "You deceived me!"

Bewildered, the believer asked, "What are you talking about?"

The new believer opened his Bible to Hebrews and said, "I've been reading the New Testament through, like you told me to do, and I just read: 'For the word of God is living and active and sharper than any two-edged sword, and piercing as far as the division of soul and spirit, of both joints and marrow, and able to judge the thoughts and intentions of the heart. And there is no creature hidden from His sight, but all things are open and laid bare to the eyes of Him with whom we have to do.'" He then slammed his Bible shut and grinned. "You knew all along that the Bible contained God's power and that the Koran is just a dead book, like any other book. I never had a chance!"

The believer smiled and asked, "And now you'll hate me for life?"

"No," came his immediate answer, "but you have to admit that it was an unfair contest."

Take a closer look at Hebrews 4:12–13. Our gospel presentations will never convey the message with the same authority as God's Word can. The very Word of God, not my word or your word or the preacher's word, is living and sharper than a two-edged sword. When we read the Word of God, our hearts are judged for what they are. The Holy Spirit, through the reading of the Scriptures, will pierce through the outer layer of a person's phony righteousness, penetrate down into the soul and spirit of that person, and convict him or her of sin, righteousness, and judgment. The Word of God can do these things in ways that we humans, who cannot read the hearts of others, can never do.

Isaiah 55:8-11 tells this very thing:

For My thoughts are not your thoughts,
Neither are your ways My ways," declares the LORD.
"For as the heavens are higher than the earth,
So are My ways higher than your ways,
And My thoughts than your thoughts.
For as the rain and the snow come down from heaven,
And do not return there without watering the earth,
And making it bear and sprout,
And furnishing seed to the sower and bread to the eater;
So shall My word be which goes forth from My mouth;
It shall not return to Me empty,
Without accomplishing what I desire,
And without succeeding in the matter for which I sent it.

God's thoughts, as found in His Word, will do a far better job of convicting our unsaved friends than we can with our explanations of His Word. Therefore, we emphasize reading the Bible with our friends, not just giving them a gospel presentation.

Planting the seed may take only a few minutes, but growth to salvation will usually take much longer. The physical process of growth illustrates this superbly. No one expects a baby to be born within a few minutes of conception; neither would we feed a brand new baby a hamburger for supper. We know that the growth process for a new believer takes time; it may be years before he is mature in his faith. We also need to look at the act of becoming a Christian as a process. Briefly, this growth process looks thus:

Unbelief   →   Decision   →   Sanctification

Table 1 on page 25 is an expanded version.

The unbeliever starts with God's built-in knowledge of a Supreme Being. The first time he is approached with the gospel, he will probably be suspicious, which he should be, considering the number of cults in the world today. As he reads the Scriptures with you, he will progress down the chart, experiencing numerous times of conviction (the work of the Holy Spirit) that force him to make decisions. With each decision will, he comes closer to true faith in Christ. Rejection can occur anywhere along the way, which might indicate that he has not truly grasped what rejecting the gospel means.

Reading the Bible with an unbeliever offers two built-in advantages. First, it gives him time to understand the gospel, preventing his making a premature "decision." True regeneration does not occur until a person has reached the point where he recognizes his personal sin and accepts Christ in genuine repentance and faith (see table 1). Because growth takes time, we do not want to rush the process. Very few people learn things without repetition. Reading the Bible over a period of weeks or months will give the unbeliever time to process the gospel message into his thinking. The Holy Spirit will weave thoughts in and out of his mind during his daily routines, forcing him to think through the practical implications of accepting the Lord Jesus as his Savior.

Second, when he finally makes a decision, it will be based firmly on the Scriptures, not on an emotional response. Nourished by this solid foundation of Bible knowledge (especially if he has read through most of John's gospel), he will mature in his faith much faster than if a premature decision had been forced upon him.

The following paragraphs give an overview of this process from beginning a friendship to leading a Bible study. I demonstrate in chapter 2 the value of becoming true friends with those whom we long to evangelize.

Chapter 3 lays out the Lord's principles of evangelism. Because Jesus Christ had a great desire to bring people to Himself, *His relationships* with people from various walks of life and *His methods of communicating* are the ultimate examples of effective evangelism.

Knowing and using these principles as related in John's gospel can greatly improve our methods of evangelism.

Chapter 4 deals with the motivation and character of the believer who desires to witness to his friends.

Chapter 5, "Building Bridges," handles the problem of starting evangelistic conversations. Too often, we think of the right things to say after the opportunity is past. This chapter should help to overcome this problem.

Chapter 6 contains a sample conversation that has occurred many times as I have attempted to motivate my friends to read the Bible with me. This approach might be somewhat different from others in that I do not make it my goal to "share the gospel" but to convince my friends to read the Bible with me.

A detailed explanation of conversational strategy follows in chapter 7. You will find ten principles for evangelism, which I believe the Lord used.

People have often asked me, "How do you witness to strangers?" Chapter 8 answers this question with a sample conversation and two additional principles.

Chapter 9 summarizes the twelve principles from chapters 6–8.

The cults have been confronting Christians in increasing numbers over the past few decades. Chapter 10 suggests a number of principles that should help you to evangelize a cult member aggressively without *being* aggressive.

Chapter 11 is a reference section. In it you will find dozens of questions, comments, objections, and responses to those questions and objections grouped into specific categories. This section could be read in an hour or so, but if you will take the time to think through these responses until you understand their ramifications, you will be well on your way to avoiding the embarrassing situation reported at the beginning of this chapter.

After you have convinced a friend to read the Bible with you, you will find in chapter 12 additional suggestions on how to "lead" an evangelistic Bible study. I say "lead," because the methods for leading an evangelistic Bible study are no different from the ones you used to motivate a friend to read the Bible with you.

Table 1. Salvation Growth Processes[2]

God's role	Believer's role	Man's response
A. INITIAL SALVATION—saved from the penalty of sin; becoming a baby believer		
General revelation (Rom. 1:18-20)	"Pluck up, break down, destroy, overthrow" (Jer. 1:10)	-8 Awareness of Supreme Being, but no effective knowledge of gospel
Conviction (John 16:8-11)	Proclamation (Acts 1:8)	-7 Initial awareness of gospel
		-6 Awareness of gospel fundamentals
		-5 Awareness of gospel implications
Regeneration	Persuasion (Acts 18:4)	-4 Positive attitude toward gospel
		-3 Recognition of personal sin
		-2 Decision to act
		-1 Repentance and faith in Christ (John 1:12; 1 John 1:9)
		0 New creature
B. GROWTH SALVATION—saved from the power of sin; becoming a mature believer		
Sanctification (1 Thess. 4:3)	Follow-up, "build, plant" (Jer. 1:10)	+1 Assurance of salvation (1 John 5:11-13)
	Discipleship	**Initial growth:** +2 "Milk of the Word"(1 Peter 2:1-3)
		Stable growth: (Col. 2:6-7) +3 "Firmly rooted"
		+4 "Built up"
		+5 "Established"
		Reproduction growth: +6 "Spiritual fruit" (Gal. 5:22-23; 2 Tim. 3:17)
		+7 "Witnesses" (Acts 1:8; John 15:1-8)
		+8 "Training" (2 Tim. 2:2)
C. COMPLETE SALVATION—saved from the presence of sin; being with Christ in eternity		

Many people will not want to read the Bible with you, but all is not lost. Chapter 13 shows you how to keep a door open to these people until a future time when they may change their mind.

Chapter 14 draws some conclusions before launching the reader into chapter 15, in which I have written out the questions and answers I have used in numerous evangelistic home Bible studies of the first six chapters of John. Chapter 16 goes the next step and answers the question, "What do I do with my friend after he or she accepts the Lord?"

DO IT!

1. Begin praying *now* for *one* unsaved friend with whom you can start reading John's gospel.
2. Begin reading John's gospel and asking yourself the following questions:
    - What would my unsaved friend think about this verse?
    - What question could I ask that would help my friend understand this verse?

Chapter 2

Come and See!

The Need for Friendship Evangelism

Friendship evangelism has been going on for hundreds of years. When John the Baptist told two of his disciples that Jesus was the Lamb of God, they asked Jesus where He lived. He told them, "Come and see." He didn't whip out the Old Testament and prove to them on the spot that He was the Messiah. For three years, Jesus demonstrated His messiahship through His actions. The disciples came to faith in Christ by observing, day and night for two to three years, how He lived as a human being.

The Lord Jesus did not give us a manual titled *How to Evangelize* filled with rules for winning people to Himself. On the contrary, we learn to evangelize by watching Him do it in everyday, live situations.

He illustrated His concern for people by serving them. He spent most of His time with the common people, healing their sicknesses, restoring their relationships, crying with them, and rejoicing with them. He became involved in their lives before He taught them.

Showing concern for neighbors or friends at work prepares them to receive the Lord's message. Their openness to the gospel may occur only through our involvement in their lives. Simply putting a welcome mat at the front door of our church building is not enough. For their sake, we need to become interested in something in which they are interested.

My wife, Christine, demonstrated this principle when she asked Martha, a young university student, if she would help Christine learn German. After a few weeks, Christine began helping Martha with her English. They developed a friendship and met together weekly for many months. Martha would take no payment for her tutoring, so we made it a habit to invite her for supper each week. During one of these meals, we began talking about the Bible and why we read it. That conversation lasted for three hours.

As she prepared to leave, I asked, "What do you think of us?"

"Well," she began slowly, "if we had had this conversation eight months ago, when we first met, I would have thought you were both crazy."

"Are we crazy?" I asked.

Her answer was surprising, "No, I've gotten to know you and you're normal, just like everyone else."

Along this same line, a Swiss missionary I know says, "If people get to know you as a nice person and then they discover that you're a bit odd about religion, they won't mind. But if all they know about you is that you're a fanatic about religion, they probably won't ever make the effort to discover that you're a nice person."

There are two reasons for becoming involved in the lives of others: so they will know that we care about them and so we can get to know them. The Lord "knew what was in man" because he could read man's heart (John 2:25). As a result, He could speak directly to the issue in each individual case. Because we can't "read hearts," we need to spend time with our unsaved friends and neighbors, talking to them about themselves, so we can eventually know how they think. This might take a few days or even months of letting them see us live Christianity before we talk to them about it.

"But how can I make friends with some of my unsaved acquaintances?" you might ask. Making friends means exhibiting an interest in others. They need to know that you have something in common with them and that you enjoy spending time with them. This can become fun. Think of things that you enjoy doing. For example:

- Go sailing or fishing or clothes shopping.
- Play or watch various sports, such as football, basketball, or soccer.
- Participate in clubs, such as amateur radio, computer, photography, astronomy, or sewing.
- Sign up for a class at a local college, whether for a hobby, a craft, or serious study.
- Offer to baby-sit for a mother with young children (or even teenagers!).
- Invite *unsaved* people to your home for a meal, coffee, or an evening of board games.

Above all, be hospitable!

After you have arrived at an idea that suits you, then ask yourself, "How can I do these things with my friends?" Then do it!

A number of our acquaintances became our friends because I invited them out for coffee after a class at the university. Later, we invited them over for tea or dinner. This led to a return invitation to their apartments. The first few times, we simply talked about them and any common interests we discovered. After a while, sometimes weeks or even months later, I brought up the subject of spiritual things. (We will have more to say about *how* to do this later.)

Many of our acquaintances became our friends through other friends. As we got to know some people well, they would naturally invite their friends to meet us. We never really had to push them to do this. It took place automatically. This, in turn, eventually led to a number of evangelistic Bible studies.

We found that we enjoyed getting to know our unsaved acquaintances as people—real, live human beings who had feelings, plans, dreams, and problems. Many of them were curious as to why we were showing an interest in them. Most of them were lonely and very open to our friendship.

One word of warning: Beware of the temptation to view non-Christians only as potential converts, whom you will cast off if they do not get saved. Friendship is sacred, and even in the hour of His betrayal, Jesus never ceased to offer His friendship to Judas. If we live our lives according to God's Word, and really challenge others to consider following it themselves, they will eventually make a choice. Either they will respond positively or *they* will walk away from the friendship.

Making friends can be easy and enjoyable, but you will probably have to spend less time with your Christian friends, and they might not understand for two reasons. First, because we have to spend so much time in the working world, we enjoy our Christian fellowship, as we should. It refreshes us and gives us strength to go back out into the fight (see Eph. 6:12). If we spend all of our time with other believers, however, we will never be able to show our unsaved neighbors and work colleagues that they, too, are important to us.

Second, some Christian circles have built up a false sense of spirituality in which separation from the world means no interaction with it whatsoever. They cut themselves off completely from all non-Christians and all "unspiritual activities" (such as sports and clubs) and condemn others who do not do the same. They lay human rules of spirituality on themselves, calling it separation from the world and thereby effectively cutting off any chance of reaching the unsaved.

"How can you go to the student cafeteria to meet her? They serve beer there!" This statement demonstrates the misconception that a Christian can somehow be contaminated by the presence of alcohol. This line of thinking eliminates all of your fine restaurants, supermarkets, and many places of clean amusement that serve food (e.g., bowling alleys).

"How can we invite our neighbors over? They smoke and our house will stink for days!" Keep an ashtray around. You can open the windows after they have left—for the sake of the gospel. Are material possessions more important than souls? (It also helps to burn a candle the whole evening while your guests are smoking.)

"What if they invite me to go somewhere with them, such as to a film that I don't think I should see? I might offend them if I turn them down." How about a creative alternative? "Well, thanks for thinking of me. I'd rather not see that film, but how about meeting me next week to ——?" (Fill in the blank with *swim, attend a concert, go to a football game,* etc.)

"But what if I do go out with a friend, or I am invited over for a meal, and they offer me a beer or a glass of wine?" If your personal convictions prohibit you from drinking any alcoholic beverages, there is nothing wrong with simply stating that you don't care for alcoholic drinks. Try saying "Could I have some juice or a soft drink instead?" I asked for a glass of milk once, and my friend asked me if I was an athlete in training! However, if all you drink is organic carrot juice, and they offer you a cola, perhaps it's time for you to make a sacrifice (see 1 Cor. 9:19).

You need to think these questions through ahead of time, so that you are not caught off guard. Ensure, however, that your convictions are based on Scripture, not upon some un-written laws of spirituality. For example, never tell your friends, "Oh, I don't smoke or drink because I'm a Christian." Many non-Christians do not smoke or drink alcohol, but they are not doing it because of Christianity. Simply tell them that you prefer not to smoke or to drink alcoholic beverages. They will respect that explanation.

It is imperative to get involved in the lives of those we want to reach for the Lord. God did not sit in heaven and demand that we come to Him, but He became one of us, yet without sin (see Heb. 4:15). We need to "become one of them," yet without sin.

Paul the Apostle wrote to the Corinthians, "I wrote you in my letter not to associate with immoral people; I did not at all mean with the immoral people of this world, or with covetous and swindlers, or with idolaters; for then you would have to go out of the world" (1 Cor. 5:9-10). Paul was warning them against immoral believers, whose behavior is tolerated by the church in the hope that ignored behavior will simply disappear. Many Christian groups, however, turn this teaching around. They

permit a believer to continue in sin while insisting that the believers separate themselves totally from all unbelievers.

On the contrary, we need to open up our lives and invite
unsaved friends to "come and see" Christianity as we live it
every day. This idea might be hard to accept at first, especially
because unbelievers can be very unlike those in our circle of
Christian friends.

In her book *Out of the Saltshaker,*[1] Rebecca Manley Pippert
tells the story of an older deacon who had ushered people into
their seats for years. One day, a young man entered the church
at the beginning of the service, just when the deacon was escort-
ing someone else down the aisle. The young man wore no shoes;
he had long, unkempt hair; and his clothes were ragged and
dirty. He entered the auditorium, walked all the way to the
front, and sat down on the floor in front of the podium. When
the deacon returned to close the front door, he noticed the
young man sitting up front. Anxiety spread throughout the
congregation.

What would the deacon say to the young man? The deacon
closed the sanctuary doors and walked down the aisle. When he
reached the front, the deacon took his own shoes off and sat
down next to the young man on the floor. There was not a dry
eye in the church that morning.

C. S. Lewis wrote the following:

> It is a serious thing to live in a society of possible gods
> and goddesses, to remember that the dullest and most
> uninteresting person you talk to may one day be a crea-
> ture which if you saw it now, you would be strongly
> tempted to worship or else a horror and a corruption
> such as you now meet, if at all, only in a nightmare. . . .
> There are no ORDINARY people. You have never met a
> mere mortal. . . . But it is immortals whom we joke with,
> work with, marry, snub, and exploit—immortal horrors
> or everlasting splendors. . . .[2]

DO IT!

1. No matter what the disguise looks like, a human being is one of the most holy objects we will ever meet. Pick out *one* unsaved aquaintance with whom you would like to become friends. Ask yourself the following questions:
    *   How can I show a personal interest in this person?
    *   How can I show this person that I care about him or her?
    *   What can I do *for* this person?
    *   What can I do *with* this person?
2. What restrictions do you have that might block your friendship with your unsaved acquaintances? Are these restrictions based on Scripture, or are they merely cultural or traditional? Are you willing to give up your cultural and traditional restrictions to have a chance of winning your friend to Christ?

Chapter 3

The Master Evangelist

The Lord's Principles for Friendship Evangelism

Now that you have made a couple of friends (or at least one!), the following questions arise:

- "What do I do with them now?"
- "How can I start a conversation about God or the Bible without offending them or scaring them off?"

The answers can be given in one sentence: Use the Lord's method to make your friend curious. Let's look at how Jesus did this.

As we proceed, I will ask questions about the Bible text with which we will be dealing. Try to answer these questions before reading further.

In John 2:13-25, Jesus entered the temple in Jerusalem and found the leaders selling sheep, doves, and oxen. The quiet serenity of the temple had been replaced by a din of animal noises; the fragrant scent of incense oils had been smothered by animal smells; the excitement of coming to the living God in an attitude of repose and worship was a ghost of the past. The moneychangers sat plying their trade. They changed the people's money and greedily took a cut from the exchange. The priests paraded their importance as a sign of spirituality.

According to the Law of Moses, to receive forgiveness for their sins, the people who came to worship needed to offer sacrifices to God. However, in Jesus' time, when a devout Jew brought the required animal to the temple, to be sacrificed, he immediately ran into a problem. The priest at the door examined the animal and, more often than not, claimed that the animal was not good enough. He should know. He had studied "Lamb Theology." The lamb would have a blemish or a defect, unseen by its owner, that did not meet the priest's standards of perfection. The priest then offered to buy the animal at a price well below its true value and then sell one of his own "perfect" animals to the man.

Where did the priest get his "perfect" animals? From a previous worshiper!

What sort of God were His priestly representatives portraying to the common Jew by such a practice? Over the centuries, since the time of their return from captivity, the Jews had fostered a picture of a God who took and took. Religion was pure business. The religious leaders had given the people a wrong picture of God because the leaders themselves did not know the living God.

Is the true God a god who only takes and takes? How do religious leaders today portray God? Do people in our time have a right or a wrong picture of the true God? What must be corrected in the thinking of many people? How can we correct this wrong thinking? How did the Lord correct it?

Jesus reacted to this temple scene. He took time to make a scourge of cords. We can almost imagine the Lord thinking through what He was going to do as He made the scourge. His anger was not like ours—selfish, hasty, and misguided. His was a well-thought-out, righteous anger.

Can we imagine the Lord entering the temple and saying, "May I have your permission to turn over this table and send all of the money flying?" Or, "Now, people, please don't do this.

Look at the mess that the animals are making all over the floor! God is going to be very upset about this!" His actions were not "polite" as most people would define *politeness* today. He did not reason with the leaders to get them to stop portraying God as the great businessman in the sky. He just cleaned house.

Can you hear the cows bellowing as the Lord laid that scourge across their backsides, the doves screeching as He opened their cages and turned them upside down, the sheep bleating, and the tables crashing down? Can you see the money flying all around the room and the priests scrambling for cover toward the back of the temple to get out of the way of a very strong, angry man—wanting to retrieve their money, but not wanting to come under that scourge? After the bedlam had quieted down a little, the priests, hidden behind the furniture, stuck their heads out and asked, "Do you have permission to do this?"

Did the Lord want to lead these priests to the Father? Then why was He so impolite to them? What kind of evangelism was that? He certainly did not seem to worry about whether His impoliteness would turn them off. Would they have listened if He had used any other approach? Apparently, Jesus did not think so.

The conversation following this scene can teach us a lot. The priests asked what sign Jesus could show them to prove that He had the right to clean their temple. The Lord said, "Destroy this temple, and in three days I will raise it up." The leaders responded, "It took forty-six years to build this temple, and will you raise it up in three days?" And that was the end of the conversation!

What can we learn from this very short story? First, Jesus did something that the leaders did not understand. He cleansed the temple. He gave them no warning, nor did He ask for their opinion or permission. This action caused them to ask Him a question. Second, when they asked Him the question, He gave them an answer that they *could not* understand, and they *did not* understand, as their response shows. Third, Jesus *did not explain* what He meant! Do you see the principles yet?

The Lord wanted to correct the Jews' wrong picture of God. He wanted to show them what God is really like—the true God (John 1:18). In contrast to the greediness of the religious leaders in the temple, how did Jesus show them that God does not take, but rather gives?

The Lord's response to Nicodemus and the Samaritan woman gives us a direct answer to this question. What did Jesus say to Nicodemus in John 3:16? ("For God so loved the world, that He *gave* His only begotten Son.") What did the Lord say to the woman at the well in John 4:10? ("If you knew the gift of God, and who it is who says to you, 'Give Me a drink,' you would have asked Him, and He *would have given* you living water.") Did He treat Nicodemus and the Samaritan woman the same way He treated the Pharisees? Let's look at Nicodemus in John 3.

What was Nicodemus's social status? He had everything this world had to offer—prestige, wealth, and power. When a man has everything, he has no reason to fear anyone. Why, then, did Nicodemus come to Jesus at night? He told Jesus, "We know that You have come from God as a teacher; for no one can do these signs that You do unless God is with him." Who did he mean by *we*? Apparently some of the Pharisees acknowledged that Jesus' miracles demonstrated His connection with the Father. Jesus made no reference to this polite, positive statement from Nicodemus. He simply said, "Unless one is born again , he cannot see the kingdom of God."

Nicodemus, as a leader of the Jews, probably knew the Old Testament, as well as all of the commentaries on it, inside out.

Jesus talked about being "born again." Where does this concept occur in the Old Testament? Ezekiel 36:25-26 talks about a new heart and a new spirit, but it says nothing about being "born again." If the Old Testament says nothing about this new birth, then how could Nicodemus have understood the Lord's comment?

We can answer this question by asking another one. Did Nicodemus understand what Jesus said? No, and the Lord continued to make statements that were incomprehensible to Nicodemus!

What was Nicodemus's response to the Lord's comments about being born of water and spirit and about a born-again person being like the wind? "How can these things be?" (v. 9).

Did Jesus answer this question? Yes, in verses 14–15. His answer is based on a passage in the Old Testament, Numbers 21, which Nicodemus could easily understand. Something comes before the Lord's answer, however. Jesus asked Nicodemus a rhetorical question in verse 10: "Are you the teacher of Israel, and do not understand these things?"

How did this question strike Nicodemus? We're not sure because his reaction is not recorded for us, but if we emphasize different words in the question, perhaps we can understand the tone of the Lord's question.

- "Are *you* the teacher of Israel and do not understand these things?"
- "Are you *the teacher* of Israel and do not understand these things?"
- "Are you the teacher of *Israel* and do not understand these things?"
- "Are you the teacher of Israel and do *not understand* these things?"
- "Are you the teacher of Israel and do not understand *these* things?"

Get the picture? It was not a polite question meant for pleasant conversation.

The biting sharpness of the question went right to the heart of Nicodemus's problem. The Pharisees claimed to be the mediators between God and man. Jesus attacked Nicodemus in his stronghold. He called into question his ability as a teacher and a mediator between God and man. The most basic and most important question that anyone could ask was, "What must a person do to get into heaven [enter the kingdom of God]?" And Jesus told Nicodemus that if he couldn't even answer this question, then he was a complete failure. What a devastating remark!

Why did Jesus treat Nicodemus thus? Do we notice any similarities or differences between this story and the previous one about Jesus in the temple? Jesus states something that Nicodemus could not understand, and Nicodemus didn't understand it. This lack of understanding caused Nicodemus to ask a question. Jesus made two more statements that Nicodemus didn't understand. Did the Lord know all along that Nicodemus wouldn't understand his comments?

After arousing Nicodemus's curiosity with statements that were *not* understandable, Jesus verbally slapped him in the face with an insulting rhetorical question. Why?

Then, and only then, did the Lord give Nicodemus an answer based on the Old Testament that he could understand. The Lord did much the same thing with the Jews in the temple. He insulted their authority and aroused their curiosity by cleansing the temple, and then He gave to their question an answer that they could not understand. In their case, however, He gave them no explanation as to what He meant. With Nicodemus, He insulted him and then gave him an answer. Why did the Lord give an answer to Nicodemus but not to the Jews?

The Samaritan woman received a little different treatment by the Lord, but the principles remain the same. Looking at John 4:7, we notice that the Lord said to her, "Give Me a drink." Was there anything unusual about this request? As we see from her response, she was surprised that Jesus, a Jew, would even speak to her, a Samaritan (and a woman at that!), let alone ask her for help. Then Jesus made a statement in verse 10 about living water.

If someone were to ask us to describe the different characteristics that water could assume, we might say that water can be hot, cold, running, polluted, wet, and so one. But what does "living water" look like? Does it have four legs and a head, or leaves like a tree? Plants, animals, and humans are living—but water? As the woman understood immediately, Jesus did not mean drinkable water as opposed to "dead" polluted water. The water in Jacob's well was drinkable, but Jesus was not referring to that. Did the woman understand what Jesus meant? Obviously not. Jesus continued to make statements that were incomprehensible, until the woman asked for the water for herself. The Lord then placed a condition before her. She was to call her husband. In this the Lord showed her that He knew her and what her life was like (vv. 17-18).

The woman's response can be evaluated in one of two ways. She might have been attempting to change the topic by shifting the conversation to a theological level and discussing one of the hottest questions between the Jews and the Samaritans: the proper location for worship, Jerusalem or Mount Gerazim. She might have been reacting to the Lord's comments about her immoral lifestyle by hiding behind theology. He countered this attempt by correcting her wrong views, but He did not allow Himself to be drawn off into a heated argument about a matter of secondary importance. He told her that a true worshiper of God worships in spirit and truth. She then told Him what she knew about the Messiah (v. 25). Then, and only then, and on the basis of this "confession," did the Lord give a direct and clear answer: "I who speak to you am He."

On the other hand, the woman might have been searching for God all of her life, only in the wrong place—husbands! Scripture teaches that husbands cannot take the place of God in a woman's life. Peter tells us that a woman must first trust God and then submit to her husband, not the other way around (1 Peter 3:5).

Because the woman now believed that she had met a true prophet, she asked Him where she could find God, in Jerusalem or in Samaria. The Lord responded by telling her that geography played no part in finding God, but only the Spirit and Truth. She then referred to her knowledge of the Messiah, and the Lord revealed Himself to her.

Are we beginning to see the Lord's principles of evangelism?

First he *aroused their curiosity*. How? He *did something* that was *not understandable* to them—cleaning the temple, asking for a drink of water—or He *made statements* that were incomprehensible to them:

- "Destroy this temple, and in three days I will raise it up."
- "Unless one is born again, he cannot see the kingdom of God."
- "If you knew the gift of God, and who it is who says to you, 'Give Me a drink,' you would have asked Him, and He would have given you living water."

This strategy is a far cry from most of our past attempts at evangelism. Our thinking usually goes something like this: I want to witness to my friend, neighbor, or relative, but once I mention the subject of God or the Bible, I'll never be able to talk to them again about it. They'll reject me and turn me off, and it will be the end of the relationship. So, my only hope is to get them to listen to the *whole* gospel in this one shot.

What happens? We attack them with everything about sin and hell and love and God and death and resurrection and sanctification and justification and propitiation and—sure enough, they never want to speak to us again! We had only the one shot. We knew all along that it would happen that way. And if someone were to suggest to us that maybe we should have insulted them first and then only given them a small tidbit of the gospel, well, that is simply ridiculous! (It does sound rather odd, doesn't it?)

This leads us to the second principle of evangelism, which the Lord followed explicitly, even with His disciples: *He did not give answers* until they were *ready* for them. The Jews in the temple never did get an answer or explanation to the Lord's statement about raising up the temple again. Nicodemus got his answer, but not until the Lord had pointed out that Nicodemus's knowledge was useless because it was not coupled with a personal relationship with the God of the Old Testament. Jesus scorned and ridiculed those who claimed to teach about God and yet did not know Him.

The woman at the well also received an answer but not until the Lord had forced her to admit her sinful lifestyle and state her belief about the coming Messiah.

How can we expect our unsaved friends to see their need of

salvation when they do not understand from what they need to be saved—sin and their own sinful nature?

Nicodemus's problem was the pride of his profession and position—knowledge and degrees. The Lord attacked him directly, as He did most of the other Pharisees. The Samaritan woman had rejected God's standard of morality. The Lord led her to see herself and who He was.

The principles of evangelism remained the same in both cases:

1. curiosity is aroused;
2. the problem is pointed out; and then (maybe),
3. the answer is given.

The methods for following these three steps differed, however. Why? Jesus chose His methods based upon the person's willingness to receive the answer. Jesus said to Nicodemus, ". . . you do not receive our witness" (John 3:11), ". . . and you are unwilling to come to Me, that you may have life" (John 5:40). If they were not willing to listen, then they either didn't get an answer or they got a parable (Mark 4:11-12). The Lord was simply using excellent teaching techniques. He did not give an answer until He had helped the person to ask the right question.

In applying this principle to our methods of evangelism, we should determine people's willingness to accept the gospel before giving them the whole package. How can we determine this? *Ask them if they want to read the Bible with you.* How to handle their objections to this question will be dealt with in the next chapter, but let's be clear on one point: If they aren't willing to read the Bible with you, they probably won't believe what you say *about* the Bible either. Look for people who will read the Bible with you and not just talk about it.

The Lord continued to use this principle with His disciples. Just a few hours before His death, He still did not give them all the answers they wanted. "I have many more things to say to you, but you cannot bear them now" (John 16:12). Verse 13 says that the apostles needed to be guided into truth, not plunged in all at once. If you wanted to learn to swim, you wouldn't want your swimming instructor to take you out into the middle of the lake and throw you overboard. This is true for our unsaved friends as well.

We do not want to give our friends the answers until we are certain that they are really searching, and we don't want to give them too many answers too quickly. An illustration that has helped me grasp these principles concerns the building of a house. Suppose that a friend of yours buys a piece of land with a house on it, but you don't think that the house is right for him. You think that he should build a different kind of house in which to live. How would you go about getting him to build a different house?

You would first have to convince him that the old house is not right for him. You would mention things that would begin to raise doubts in his mind about the old house. The ventilation is out-dated, and the walls are starting to lean outward. The chimney is clogged and could start a bad fire. The final blow comes when you show him its crumbling foundation. You take him around to the back of the house, reach down, pull out one brick, and say, "How many bricks would I need to pull out before the house collapses to the ground? How many do I have to pull out before you will be convinced that your foundation is rotten?"

The easiest way to destroy his house would not be to start taking off the roof but by removing a few key bricks (cornerstones) from the foundation and letting the house collapse under its own weight.

The same is true in witnessing. Most people can assimilate only so much information at one time. Therefore, we give them the gospel a little at a time. Very few people react favorably to being bombarded with the gospel all at once. They don't like feeling that you have used the machine gun or shotgun approach, filling them with gospel bullet holes and leaving them stunned, if not dead.

Do you like having someone push his or her view of something down your throat, giving you no time to think it through and demanding that you make an immediate decision? Neither does anyone else.

The first step toward bringing a person to Christ is to make him doubt his own values and self-established goals. Eventually he has to realize his sin before a holy God.

One man told me, after he had come to the Lord in one of our Bible studies, "I never realized how wrong my thinking was. You showed me, a little at a time, how wrong my whole outlook on life was."

When a person has come this far, the next step rests on his shoulders. He will ask himself, "Am I willing to admit my sin to God? Am I willing to change my thinking?" The infinitive *to repent* in the New Testament means "to change one's thinking." By taking enough bricks from his philosophical foundation, you will have helped him face the question of repentance.

God told Jeremiah to use this principle of destruction first and then reconstruction. "See, I have appointed you this day over the nations and over the kingdoms, to pluck up and to break down, to destroy and to overthrow, to build and to plant" (Jer. 1:10). He used four words for destruction followed by two words for construction. Destroying an old thought pattern often requires more work than building a new one. Why? Willingness. Once the old pattern is destroyed, a person is open and ready to accept God's way of looking at things. Look again at table 1 in chapter 1.

Paul relates the same principles in 2 Corinthians 10:3–5. "For though we walk in the flesh, we do not war according to the flesh, for the weapons of our warfare are not of the flesh, but divinely powerful for the destruction of fortresses. We are destroying speculations and every lofty thing raised up against the knowledge of God, and we are taking every thought captive to the obedience of Christ." We are involved in a battle of the mind: the world's and the Devil's views of things versus God's view of things. We have to help people change their thinking.

Our goal is to make our friends curious enough to want to read the Bible with us.

Door-to-door and tract evangelism can be quite effective in some cultures, and we need little preparation for these methods, just a time slot in our weekly schedule. However, the Lord's method of making people curious and getting them into His Word is quite different from our past hit-and-run methods. To make people curious, we need to make certain adjustments to our thinking.

The apostle Paul approached different types of people with different arguments in Romans 1-3. When dealing with the godless, immoral person in Romans 1:18-32, Paul referred to the knowledge of God as evidenced in His creation. He did not immediately open the Bible and hit this type of individual with a dozen Bible verses. This type of person rejects the Bible in the first place, and when we do this to our godless friends, the conversation stops and goes no further.

The second type of person—the moral, good-deed-oriented person—requires a different tactic. This person will say such things as, "I'm a good, moral person. I'm just as good as, if not better than, the next person, and I'm certainly better than the guy Paul describes in Romans 1:18-32. If anybody else gets into heaven, I have a right to go there, too."

Paul does not refer to the heavens or the Bible, but he points out the discrepancy between this individual's attitude toward others ("I'm as good as the next person," Rom. 2:1-4) and his lifestyle. Paul says that this person condemns others for their actions, yet he does the same things. Paul points out the inconsistencies in the lifestyle of people like this and then asks them if they really believe God is going to judge others but let them off the hook. I believe that the majority of our non-Christian friends fit into this second category.

With the third type of individual, the religious person, Paul goes directly to the Bible and attacks them with the very standard they claim to possess—the Word of God.

"But I don't know how to make people curious," you might say at this point. "I wouldn't know where to begin. I don't know how to turn a conversation around toward spiritual things. And when my friends do start talking about such things, I don't think fast on my feet, and I never have the right answers to their questions or objections."

Let me assure you that the art of making people curious *can be learned!* This technique is not only for gifted evangelists. It has been learned and used by believers with many different personalities. At a conference for church leaders, one man told the group, "Everyone knows that I do not have the gift of evangelism, but ever since I've been using these principles, I've been reading the Bible with friends and leading them to the Lord regularly for the last eight years." We have taught a number of people to use these principles, and the more you practice using the conversations in the chapters to follow, the better you will get.

In the next chapter, we will discuss some things that are necessary for learning this process.

DO IT!

1. Read John 5 and ask yourself, "Why didn't Jesus heal every person at the pool? What was the main purpose of the Lord's miracles?"
2. Read John 9, and ask yourself, "Why did the Lord tell the man to go to the pool and wash his eyes, when He did not use the pool in chapter 5 to heal the sick man? What did the Lord want to accomplish by *sending* the man to the pool instead of *taking* him to the pool?"
3. What major sins do you see in your unsaved friend (e.g., pride, immorality, or lying)? What *questions* (not accusations!) can you ask your friend that will point out these areas as wrong? Would you ever insult your friend to get him to think about his sin, God, or the Bible?
4. Write down five different questions that will make your unsaved friend think that his sin or his views about God and the Bible might be wrong. Then use these questions the next time you meet him!

Chapter 4

The Apprentice's Preparation

Our Preparation for Friendship Evangelism

Regular, personal Bible study remains an essential. Our friends have to see that we know something about the topic of which we are talking. Think about the following italicized words in Acts 4:13, "Now as they [the Jewish religious leaders] observed the *confidence* of Peter and John, and understood that they were *uneducated and untrained men,* they were marveling, and began to recognize them as *having been with Jesus.*" Peter and John's confidence did not depend on their theological degrees from the local Jerusalem Bible College. They had been with the Lord Jesus. That was enough to amaze the religious leaders of their day. And it's enough to amaze our friends today.

We have the same opportunity to meet Him in his Word. "Jesus answered and said to him, 'If anyone loves Me, he will keep My word; and My Father will love him, and We will come to him, and make Our abode with him'" (John 14:23). It should be obvious that "keeping" the Lord's Word means something different from storing it on the bookshelf to be dusted off at Christmas and Easter. Our friends must see our own confidence in God's Word if they are to take us seriously. If we are dummies when it comes to our knowledge of God's Word, there is no better time to start changing that situation than now. The religious leaders saw Peter and John's "confidence," and later (Acts 4:31) Peter and John spoke the Word of God with "boldness." The more you study John's gospel, the more confident you will become in your own faith.

Please keep in mind that you are doing this primarily for the Lord, not just for yourself or your friends. Second Timothy 2:15 makes this quite clear: "Be diligent to present yourself *approved to God* as a workman who does not need to be ashamed, handling accurately the word of truth." Our commitment is to the Lord Himself. This book is not meant for those who think that personal Bible study and evangelism are simply time-filling hobbies.

Sincerity

On the other hand, we won't have all of the answers to their questions, but that will make very little difference. Our main objective centers on convincing our friends that we do not have all of the answers; therefore, they have to learn to find the answers for themselves!

Please keep in mind that we are not going to save anyone. The Holy Spirit through the Word of God will do that, as John tells us in John 16:8–11. Hebrews 4:12 cannot be stressed enough: "For the word of God is living and active and sharper than any two-edged sword, and piercing as far as the division of soul and spirit, of both joints and marrow, and able to judge the thoughts and intentions of the heart." It is not "my word," "your word," or "the preacher's word" that is living and active and sharper than any two-edged sword. Sometimes our words are sharper than a sword, but usually in the wrong way. Our job is simply to get our friends to read the Bible with us and let them find the answers to their questions for themselves.

Give them as few answers as possible. Although you know the Bible better than they do (you've been reading it regularly, haven't you?), and they know that you know the Bible better than they do, they must come to see that you are not their answer person. The answers are in the Bible. If they want them, they will have to search the Scriptures for themselves to find them. You are willing to guide them in their search, but you are not "clergy." You will need to repeat over and over again that they can understand the basics of knowing God as easily as you or anyone else can—if they *want* to understand them.

Remember: Our job is to bring our friends to the *Lord* in His Word, and then He brings them to *faith* in His person. We make the introduction; He saves them.

In practice, this type of evangelism works better at first between just two friends. Don't try to reach your whole neighborhood. When Andrew met the Lord, he didn't organize an evangelistic campaign; he went and told his brother. Pick out one friend and get to know her better. Become interested in her as a person. Give her time. Don't go too far too fast.

As she gets to know you, she will begin to see that you are different. She will eventually ask you why you act the way you do, and then you can apply 1 Peter 3:15: "But sanctify Christ as Lord in your hearts, always being ready to make a defense to every one who asks you to give an account for the hope that is in you." The more you make Christ Lord of your life and the center of all your activities, the more you will stand out as being different from your friends. Your different lifestyle will be the biggest factor in making them curious about the gospel.

An acquaintance of mine testifies to this principle when he relates his testimony. He met a young lady at a party one evening and was drawn to her because of her smile. As everyone was leaving, he asked her if she was interested in spending the evening with him in his apartment. Without sounding horrified, the young lady simply smiled at him and announced that she did not need that kind of a relationship. Surprised at her response, he asked her what she meant. She replied that she had a personal relationship with Jesus Christ, and he provided all the relationship and meaning she would ever need. He asked her if he could drop in the following day, and she said, "I've already told you I won't sleep with you."

"I know that," he answered. "I want to hear about this Jesus." She said she would agree, if she could invite a couple of male believers over as well. Within a few weeks, the young man accepted the Lord as his Savior.

Relatives seem to be the hardest to reach with the gospel. They have known you all of your life, and trying to talk them into the kingdom will almost always fail, unless you have first impressed them with a changed life.

A young student came to me at a student Bible conference a few summers ago and said that she had just become a Christian. She wanted to know how she could talk her mother into becoming a Christian as well. After talking to her for a few minutes, I detected that she harbored some bitterness toward her mother. I asked her if she loved her mother, and she started to cry. She said that she knew she should, and now that she had become a Christian, she wanted to work on it. Then she said, "It would be easier for me if my mother were a believer, too."

I described a hypothetical situation for her: What if she goes home and tells her mother that she (the mother) has been wrong all of her life and that her daughter has come home to set her straight? The girl thought about that for a few minutes and then said, "She's known me all my life. She'll probably ask me what I could possibly have to teach her."

I then asked her if she really wanted to lead her mother to the Lord. When she answered yes, I asked, "What is the one thing above all other things that you hate to do the most when you are at home?"

She responded with no hesitation, "I hate to wash the dishes."

I said, "If you really want to lead your mother to the Lord, then go home and volunteer to do the dishes every day for the next six months. Don't tell your mother that you've become a Christian. When she asks you how this conference went, just say it was nice. Above all, don't complain about doing the dishes and don't witness to her. Just do the dishes."

She asked me how that would help lead her mother to the Lord, but I told her that I wouldn't answer that question until she had done the dishes for six months at home. Then she could call me and tell me what happened, and I would answer her question.

Four months later, she called me to say that she had done what I had suggested and that she didn't need an answer to her question anymore. Within three months her mother had become so irritated by her daughter's cheerful dishwashing that she finally demanded to know why she had changed so much. Her daughter replied, "I've been reading the Bible, and Jesus has changed my life. Would you like to read it with me?" The mother refused but wanted to know what was in the Bible. The daughter remembered what I had said about not giving answers, and she declined to tell her mother what was in the Bible. The young student wanted to call me and tell me that she and her mother had just begun reading the gospel of John together. The mother eventually became a believer.

Prayer

Many books on prayer are available for you to read, and many seminars on prayer are offered for you to attend. The best solution for a weak prayer life, however, is simply to pray more! If you have a regular time of prayer, talk to the Lord about your unsaved friend or relative regularly. Ask other believers to pray for your friend as well. The more prayer that is offered for your friend, the better. When he gets saved, the other believers who have prayed for him will be encouraged too.

Use any system necessary to jog your memory to pray for him a number of times each day. Praying short prayers for him daily will do more for your own awareness of your need for God's help and mercy than praying just once a week at a weekly prayer meeting. More will be done through prayer than through all of our best-laid plans and methods. Pray for your friend every time you think of it.

DO IT!

1. Read Acts 4:1-13, and ask yourself, "How can I increase in confidence in my witnessing? How can I show my unsaved friend that I have been with the Lord Jesus?"

2. How can you let your unsaved friend know that you have problems, just like everyone else, but that the Lord helps you work out these problems?

3. Write down three things you could do for your unsaved relatives that would make them ask, "Why did you do that?" You want to be able to tell them you did it because you love them.

4. How can you remind yourself to pray for your friend at least three times a day?

Chapter 5

Building Bridges

How to Turn a Conversation to Spiritual Things

Moving a conversation around to spiritual things can be the most difficult part of witnessing. We can talk freely with our friends about many subjects, but are at a loss when we want to bridge the gap between everyday life and the Lord. What does driving to work every morning or playing golf or washing the dishes or changing the baby have to do with our spiritual lives? How can we make a comment based on an everyday situation that will cause our friends to ask us what we meant? How can we ask them a question (again, based on an everyday situation) that will cause their thoughts to leap into the realm of spiritual things?

Let me emphasize at this point that the ability to turn a conversation around to spiritual things is not a "gift." It can't be found in any of the gift passages in the Bible (1 Corinthians 12 and so on). But *it can be learned!* The only requirement is that you be concerned enough about the salvation of your unsaved friend to practice thinking through your own everyday situations and plan ahead what you would like to say in each situation.

The following conversation steps will guide you through the process from talking about the weather to discussing the gospel.

This process is universal. It doesn't depend on your personality. Anybody can carry on a conversation with another person using these four steps, if he or she *practices* the steps ahead of time. In fact, in some situations you will be able to go from step one to step four in just a few minutes. With long-term friends, work colleagues, or relatives, it may take you longer to get to step four, but if you practice the method beforehand, bathe it in prayer, and carry it in fear and trembling, the Lord might surprise you and allow you to get to step four with the most hardened antagonist!

Please, dear reader, learn and practice these four steps well.

The Overview

1. *Surface Talk*—Is the person alive?
    Talk about the weather, sports, and so on.

2. *Personal Talk*—Will the person open up?
    Talk about family, jobs, or interests.

3. *Religious Talk*—Is there interest in spiritual things?
    Talk about religion, churches, or church activities.

If the friend is not interested at this time, retreat to step two!

4. *Spiritual Talk*—Is the person seeking God?
    Talk about what Christ has done for you; ask his or her view of Christianity. Then invite him or her to a Bible study *or* give the gospel.

If the friend is not seeking at this time, retreat to step three!

Reality Check—Read Colossians 4:2–6.

1. *Surface talk* with our acquaintances opens the door to conversation. We do this all the time, often without knowing it.

2. *Personal talk* is the step of discovery. We want to know as much about our acquaintances as possible before moving on to more serious topics. We want our friends to open up about themselves.

3. *Religious talk* moves the conversation in the direction of the gospel. We are not going to give the gospel at this point. We have to find out if they are interested in spiritual things. Even our relatives, whom we think we know so well, may be seeking the Lord but may never have had anyone to talk to about it. This step is very important. Don't hurry on to step four, yet.

4. *Spiritual talk* will discover if our friends are seeking God or just dabbling in religious ideas. There are lots of moral people who don't want God to mess up their lives. Is the person truly seeking God, or is he happy to be just a religious person? At this point you have to decide what you want to offer your friend: the whole gospel or a Bible study. When the Lord first met people, He spent more time making them thirsty for Him than He did telling them how to get into heaven.

Let's look at these four steps in some detail.

1. Surface Talk

Have you ever stood next to a person in a shop for a few seconds and neither of you spoke? After a few more seconds, you both became uncomfortable. The reasons for this would need another book to explain, but the fact remains, you will react in one of two ways. You will either step away from that person, putting more distance between you, or you will make some comment on a variety of neutral subjects. Perhaps you will mention the weather (if we had no weather, most of us wouldn't have anything to talk about!), the slow service in the shop, the horrible rush-hour traffic, and so on.

In most cases, we talk about such things because we can't handle long periods of silence with strangers or acquaintances. This level of conversation is the perfect starting place for an evangelistic conversation. Your only goal at this point is to mention something more personal about yourself than the weather:

family, school, work, neighbors, pets, or anything that opens your life up just a little to this acquaintance. Just mention it, don't give your life story! Then, casually ask the acquaintance about that same area of his or her life. For example, after you have mentioned the weather, say,

> "Yes, I've lived here for [it doesn't matter how long], and I think that the weather is [it doesn't matter what you think about the weather]. Have you lived here long?"

Telling a person something about yourself gives you the unspoken right to ask that person the same thing. There are infinite possibilities for moving from surface talk to personal talk, as long as you remember your goal. You want people to open up about themselves. You are not interested in talking about yourself! You want to find out as much as possible about them. In order to do this effectively, you will have to *listen* to them more than you talk about yourself. As they open up a little bit, tell them a little more about yourself, and then ask them more about themselves. Most people love to talk about themselves. If you practice *listening* to people, you will make enormous progress in your evangelistic efforts.

2. Personal Talk

This level of conversation is easy. You will never run out of things to talk about. You can ask questions about a person's birthplace, hometown, family, education, work, vacations, retirement, interests and hobbies, music, artistic abilities, politics, cooking, history, and sports of all kinds. One very good subject to talk about is weekends and free time. Ours has become an entertainment society.

Once a subject has been mentioned, ask a question about it. Use the five W's: Who? What? Where? When? Why? If possible, attempt to establish some common interests with the person. Just remember, you don't have to be an expert in a field to ask someone's opinion about that subject. You just have to be a good listener. And if you don't like what the person likes, show an interest in it anyway! You are *not* trying to change his or her priorities or hobbies. You are trying to bring that person to the Lord. Ask about his or her favorite sport, even if you don't know that a basketball is round and larger than a baseball.

One very important point is to find out the person's first name and use it off and on in the conversation. A person's first name is one of the most important words in his or her vocabulary. Be genuinely interested in that person.

Throughout this level of conversation, watch the person's body language: eyebrows going up and down, eyes looking away from you, smiling or frowning, nervous tapping of feet or fingers, harsh or smooth voice tone, high or low voice pitch. You want to discover if the person is comfortable with the direction of the conversation. If the person seems to be closing up, don't feel guilty! Relax. Enjoy the practice and go find another acquaintance to talk to. If the person becomes vulgar in his vocabulary, ask yourself if this is his normal way of expressing himself or if he is trying to offend you. If this is how he normally talks, don't take offense and don't correct him. Keep *listening* and keep the conversation going. If he is trying to offend you (which is very rare at this level of conversation), start using "God talk" immediately, such as "The Bible says . . . "; "Jesus always . . ."; or "God wants us to . . . " and so on. This will usually cause him to leave.

This level of conversation is very easy to learn, especially if you will carry out a little experiment with yourself. For the next week, spend thirty minutes a day starting conversations with strangers or acquaintances about surface topics and moving on to personal items. Then *ask questions about their interests and do not talk about yourself.* Try it! You will eventually see common interests develop.

3. Religious Talk

The first levels of conversation are pre-evangelism. They're all about building rapport. Now we are going to take the plunge. But first, let's destroy a wrong assumption on our part. Most believers assume that a stranger or acquaintance does not want to talk about religious things. This is categorically wrong. Even atheists like talking about their views of God! They may be irrational, but they love a listening ear. Although most people may not respond positively toward the gospel, they do appreciate having someone ask them about themselves and listening to their ideas or their problems in life. A listening ear may be the very thing that causes a person to seek God.

If you do get to the level of religious talk, and the person seems cool or antagonistic, retreat! Back down to the personal talk level. We are not called to push the gospel on anyone. When the apostle Paul witnessed in Acts, he "reasoned" with the people (Acts 17:17); he didn't force-feed them. If a person does not want to discuss religious things, then you can't reason with that person. Go back to talking about things at the second level and keep the conversation friendly.

When you transition from surface talk to personal talk, you make a statement about yourself and then you ask the other person a question about that same area of his or her life. The transition process is the same between personal talk and religious talk. For example, when talking about how you spend your weekends, say,

> "Well, on weekends we usually [it doesn't matter what you do] on Saturday, and then we [eat out in a restaurant, have friends over for lunch, whatever] after church."

Wait a few seconds to watch for body language, then continue with,

> "Do you attend church?"

Regardless of the answer, say,

> "I see. Have you ever read the Bible?"

Regardless of the answer, say,

"You know, I'm always interested in other people's viewpoints on what's in the Bible. Would you have time for us to get together *just one time* to read a passage together? I would really appreciate listening to what you think about it."

Emphasize the "just one time" so the person can see that you are not trying to drag or seduce him or her into a lifetime cult. Here's another example:

"I really enjoy reading, especially books that make me think. What do you like to read?"

His or her answer.

"Do you ever read any philosophy or religious books?"

His or her answer.

"I see. Have you ever read the Bible?"

Regardless of the answer, say:

"You know, I'm always interested in other people's viewpoints on what's in the Bible. Would you have time for us to get together *just one time* to read a passage together? I would really appreciate listening to what you think about it."

See how *easy* that is? And if you *practice having these conversations with imaginary people*, it will really start to come more naturally. Remember your goal: getting your acquaintance to read the Bible with you just one time.

Here are some topics and bridges that can lead into religious talk.

- Ask a new person in town if he has found everything he needs, like the post office, court house, church, schools. Offer to help if he needs it.
- Ask a person in which church she was married and what kind of church it is. If the conversation continues in this direction, ask what her church believes about something, such as prayer, working on Sunday, how to get to heaven, the person of Jesus. If the opportunity arises, ask *why* her church believes what it believes. Ask her if she believes the same as her church. If you start to share your beliefs, don't preach! You might even invite her to read the Bible with you one time to compare viewpoints on it.
- Talk about the Arab-Israeli conflict and how it all started.
- Decry the decline of morals and ask if evil people will ever be punished for their deeds. (Will God judge people someday?)
- Comment on the tabloids at the checkout counter.
- Use religious holidays as springboards about the real reason for the season.
- Use God-related phrases: Thank God. God bless you.
- Use different names for God: God, the Lord, the good Lord; then later, Jesus Christ, Jesus.
- Share your own personal spiritual truth about life without preaching a sermon.
- If the other person mentions God, use his or her words as a bridge.

What do we do when our acquaintance responds with silence? Smile and back down to the previous level of conversation. People are still noticing your witness! Don't feel guilty and press harder. Don't become discouraged and quit witnessing altogether. Leave the results to God. Many people may not want to talk about religious topics. Don't fret. Just accept it and keep looking for seekers.

What do we do if the person becomes aggressive? Stay friendly and break off the conversation as politely as possible. People respond negatively for a number of reasons. They might have had a bad experience with someone pushing religious views on them, and they now associate any conversation about spiritual things with that bad experience. You can easily help them overcome this by remaining friendly and not pushing the conversation any further. You might even mention that it really bothers you when people try to push their beliefs on you! This will usually disarm them and you might be able to resume the conversation at a less tense level.

Another reason people might respond negatively is because they are under conviction and intuitively know that the conversation will show them their sin, even though you never mention sin or their lifestyle. The Holy Spirit works inside human beings in ways that we cannot understand or predict.

If you are a friendly person and are trying to back down to the previous level of conversation, a person will rarely turn seriously aggressive. But if you are verbally attacked with vulgar language, then you may experience the joy of being persecuted for your faith. Rejoice and thank the Lord for allowing you to share in His sufferings. Your witness is making an impact. "Now, Lord, look on their threats, and grant to Your servants that with all boldness they may speak Your word" (Acts 4:29 NKJV).

4. Spiritual Talk

If you have been constantly building bridges from one subject to another, you will start to notice if the person wants to proceed with the conversation. You want to ask yourself, "Does this person's actions and attitudes indicate that he or she wants to talk about spiritual things?" If you sense an openness after the religious talk, you can move to spiritual talk by going in a number of directions.

You can invite him or her to visit your church. However, this might be too threatening at first.

You can ask the person two questions:

1. "If you were to die today, could you say for certain that you will go to heaven?"

2. "Why should God let you into His heaven?" This question lets you know what the person is trusting in.

You can share the whole gospel with him or her. If you choose this route, keep the message as simple as possible, use illustrations for each point and, if the person is open to it, repeat the main points of the gospel a number of times from different angles.

You can ask the person to read the Bible with you one time to see what God has to say about the things that you have been talking about. If this approach seems a little frightening to you at the moment, then you might invite the person to an evangelistic Bible study that is being led by someone else. This approach could give you the experience you desire to lead your own study in the near future.

The previous ideas should give you plenty of comments and questions to use in your own daily circumstances as you attempt to turn a conversation toward the spiritual realm. You simply have to *practice* thinking through the four levels of conversations ahead of time. The key is to remember your immediate goal. You do not want to give them the whole gospel all at once but rather you want to make them curious about your beliefs. Following are some ideas you can use to accomplish this.

Reading

Letting people see you reading your Bible is a natural way to make them curious enough to ask what you are reading. Take your pocket New Testament everywhere with you. Pull it out and read a couple of verses when you know that people are watching you. You don't have to pull it out, read a verse, drop the Bible on the floor, and announce loudly, "Oh dear, I dropped my Bible!" Read a couple of verses at different times throughout the day: at coffee break or lunch, in the lecture hall, on the bus or the train (not while driving, which will elicit a different reaction from the one you want!). Once you have answered a curious observer with the two words *the Bible,* the door is open for you to ask, "Have you ever read it?" No matter what answer he or she gives, you can reply, "I've found the Bible to be very interesting and helpful." With a few more such comments, you can easily ask, "Would you like to read the Bible with me?"

Reading has proved to be one of the best springboards available to us. It does not matter what people read. If they like to read, you can talk about your or their reading interests.

For example, after becoming friends with a student in a class I was taking, we discovered that we both loved to read. After comparing books we had read and books we would like to read, I asked him if he liked to read a book with someone and then discuss it (or argue about it!). He said yes, so I asked him if he had ever read and discussed or argued about the Bible, and would he like to do so with me? He said that he preferred to choose a different book, so I asked if we could read two books by switching off every other week. He agreed and chose a philosophy book that nearly did me in! The outcome was that I learned a lot of philosophy—and I often complained to my wife about its uselessness—but my friend eventually received the Lord! My friend and I still laugh today about his choice and how thankful he is that I agreed. In the beginning, he did not understand the Bible, and I did not understand the philosophy book. He came to an excellent understanding of God's Word, and I learned how he thought. He will be with me in eternity.

Employment

Ask your friends the following questions or make the following statements: "Is work an end in itself? Is there more meaning to my work than just receiving a paycheck? Some people eat to live, whereas others live to eat. Does this apply in any way to our work? Have you ever wondered what God has to say about work? Do you think that God made work as punishment for man's sin? (No, He didn't! Adam was given work in the garden *before* he sinned. The *fruit* of his work became harder to obtain after the fall.) The Bible has some very interesting things to say about the one extreme of laziness versus the other extreme of working too much. Would you like to read the Bible with me to discover God's view of employment? God even says some unique things about employers. Have you ever wondered how our employment or the work we do here on earth will affect eternity?"

Hobbies and Sports

When you are watching a game (live or on TV) with your friend or playing tennis or hiking or exchanging stamps for your collections or stomping on each other's gardens while chasing down that rare butterfly, you can always build a bridge with the following statement: "I really need this time to pursue my hobby. It takes my mind off my weekly routine." Then follow up with some of the following questions: "Do you think we need rest and relaxation? Why or why not? Maybe we should always work seven days a week. Do you believe that God made us to rest or to work?"

You might ask, "Do you ever wonder where we get our different interests? Why do some people like flying kites and others weaving baskets? Is each person unique? Why or why not?"

Or, "Why do some people run from one hobby (or job) to another, never seeming to be satisfied with life? What do you think makes a person satisfied with life?" If you can get your friend to ask you if you are satisfied with life, tell him that you find satisfaction reading what God says about people in the

Bible. This theme can go in a number of profitable directions. Think through the topic ahead of time with your friend in mind (i.e., his job, his hobbies, and his satisfaction or dissatisfaction with life) and plan your questions accordingly.

Or, "Why do some people practice a sport or a hobby with a vengeance? Why do they always seem as though they have to win? Why are some people extremely competitive and others are not? What is it about people that makes them want to rule over others, even at the lower levels of society? Could you ever imagine a world without any competition?" If you are really bold, you might add, "I can imagine such a world because the Bible talks about one, one that God is going to bring to earth in the not-so-distant future." Remember, you only want to make your friend curious enough to read the Bible with you. You do not want to explain the book of Revelation to him on the front porch in twenty minutes.

History

Discussion of war and the total lack of security in this world can lead to a conversation about false hope. Many Europeans asked me what I thought about the Persian Gulf War in early 1991, and I replied, "When it's over, there will be another one somewhere else. In fact, someday there will be another one in Europe, and eventually another world war." Needless to say, they asked me how I could know that! I replied, "It's easy. First, history and human nature are clear indicators. I believe it was Goethe who once said, 'Mankind has made lots of progress, but the human being has always remained the same. The only hope for the human being is to change him on the inside.' However, almost two thousand years ago, the Bible predicted all of these things, and the Bible hasn't been wrong yet." The next obvious thing to do was to ask these friends if they have ever read the Bible and if they would like to do so with me.

False hope is another line of discussion. People have said to me, "I hope there's not another war in Europe." I ask them what grounds they see for having this hope, and this leads back to what the Bible says. Think of a number of different examples of false hope in your own realm of experience and bring the conversation around to the Bible.

Science

This subject can be approached from the viewpoint of either the scientist or the layman. In either case, our unsaved friends have to be shown the fallacy of believing every scientific theory that comes along (they will be replaced by newer ones in the near future) or thinking that scientists are gods who never make mistakes, even though many of their "conclusions" are based on extremely flimsy evidence. No *true* scientist will ever claim to have "arrived" (i.e., to have learned all there is to know about a subject) and, therefore, claim he can't be wrong in his current conclusions. Quite often, science involves more politics than searching for truth. A college biology book I had to read for a class once even made that statement about the work of some Nobel Prize winners.

Following are some thoughts to share with your unsaved friends to make them curious.

We are governed by physical laws that limit our freedom, and we do not violate these laws for our own good health. Does God have spiritual laws that we should obey for our health? You would never jump off the Golden Gate Bridge, hoping that you will go up instead of down. The results of trying to break this law of physics would be uncomfortable. Are there any uncomfortable results from breaking God's laws? How could we find an answer to this question? Will science be able to rescue the world from itself? Will more scientific progress draw humankind together? Why can't the scientists tell us where matter came from originally and how dead matter became living matter?

You can use any area of science to springboard into spiritual things, including the following.

Biology. Where did life come from originally? What is the meaning of life or of beauty? Why do humans appreciate beauty and animals don't? A human seeks meaning in a Rembrandt painting, whereas a dog might chew it up. And don't overlook the subject of cloning! If we can clone humans, where do these humans get their souls? Does God want us to clone humans? Is God forced to put a soul into each clone? What does the Bible say about everyone being made in God's image? What does that mean?

Physics and chemistry. What holds all matter together? How could such a complex system of atoms and subatomic particles be the result of sheer chance? Why are we just beginning to discover that classical mechanics is a special branch of quantum mechanics, instead of the reverse (humankind, as a life-form, being bound within very narrow limits)? How could we even hope to find God outside of our extremely limited life-support system unless God chose to come into our earthly system and reveal Himself in terms that we could understand?

The arts, humanities, social sciences, and literature and languages lend themselves quite well to starting discussions about the meaning of life, who and what we are, why we have all of the problems that have always plagued us, and so on.

If you have the chance, you might read books written by an unsaved expert in some field that would give you some insight into how the unsaved mind thinks. Next, analyze this book critically by subjecting it to the biblical viewpoint. Then talk to your friends about how you enjoyed reading the book but disagreed with the author's conclusions. Tell them how and why you disagree by referring to the Bible.

Politics

This subject can be dangerous. Remember: You are a Christian first and then a political person (Democrat, Republican, American, and so on). Winning your friend to Christ is eternally more important than getting him to change political parties.

Questions and thoughts to use include the following. "Do you think that politics will stop crime, wars, poverty, and so on? Why or why not? Why do many people become irate when discussing politics? Why do people sometimes have a hard time admitting that they are wrong? Why do people champion a cause so religiously and then change their minds later? Do you think that people who put their faith in politics all of their lives will believe that it was worth it? Does a politician want to be accepted or rejected? Why?" Chapter 7 of the gospel of John gives us an interesting view of Jesus as He acts in a manner opposite to that of the average politician. He didn't want to make Himself known, and He told people the truth about themselves.

Money

Questions and ideas to use for discussion starters about this topic include the following. "What does the statement 'The love of money is the root of all evil' mean? Why do money and material possessions sometimes bring out the worst in a person? Why is money such a touchy subject for many people? Do you know what the Bible says about money (Matthew 7 and James 5)? Does money keep people from coming to God? How? Should evangelists be rich or poor? Can a person be rich and still please God? (Yes, Abraham was rich!) What does God say should be the purpose of money?"

Sex

This subject for the braver ones must be approached with caution. The older generation will usually not appreciate the "openness" of the younger generation. Keep in mind your goal: to make unsaved friends curious enough to want to read the Bible with you.

Ideas to be discussed with your unsaved friends include the following. "Is sex an end in itself? Is sex meant just for procreation? Is it a sin to enjoy sex within marriage? (Some religions believe this!) Should we have moral standards by which to live? Who should determine these standards? Why are there so many different moral standards in the world? Does God have a moral standard for us? What happens if we reject His standard? Is pleasure the ultimate end in life? If you think it is, what if one person's pleasure hurts another human being? Should we stop people from hurting themselves even though they claim to be enjoying themselves?"

If you are a believer and are engaged, your unsaved friends will be absolutely baffled that you are not sleeping with the person to whom you are engaged. You will have many opportunities to talk about how your faith leads to such a high morality. Be brave! You have the high ground. Your unsaved friends cannot contradict you because they have never experienced such purity and self-control. And they can never again be virgins. Your purity is a very powerful testimony.

Academic Studies or School

This topic can be used with high-school as well as college students. At these ages, most young people are open to thinking about the meaning and purpose of life. Challenge them not to throw their lives away on themselves but to give them to Jesus and let Him make them into His image.

Ideas to start them thinking include the following. "Why should you go to school/college—to get a job and earn money and get married and have children who grow up and go to college to get a job while you get old and die? Where is the meaning in it all? Does the Bible have anything to say about learning? (Yes! Psalm 1; 119; Philippians 4:8; and many other Scripture references.) Are there some topics into which God forbids us to look? Why would God do that? Of the many trees in the Garden of Eden, why did God not want Adam and Eve to eat from the Tree of the Knowledge of Good and Evil? Why that specific tree? Where should human beings go to discover what is good and evil (right and wrong)? Should they seek these answers from their own experiences (and maybe damage themselves permanently, as did Adam and Eve), or should they go to God for advice?"

Housekeeping

Homemakers spend the vast majority of their time doing housework. There has to be a way to relate this responsibility to the spiritual realm. Try the following ideas with your neighboring housekeepers.

"Does life seem as meaningless as housework? A homemaker

is always doing the same things over and over again, but the work is never done. How does the phrase go? 'A woman's work is never dumb, uh, done.' The Bible has some very positive things to say about being faithful in tasks that seem never to be finished. A clean house can contribute to a happy family, but this happiness is only temporary. A fanatical house-cleaner may or may not have a happy family life. Similarly, one who is not so neat also may or may not have a happy family life. From where does true happiness come? Can a person be truly happy doing the same work day after day? The Bible also speaks a lot about contentment apart from our circumstances. Would you like to read the Bible with me to discover these things?"

Weather

If we did not have the weather to talk about, 90 percent of our time with other people would be spent in silence! Because we talk about the weather so much, it should be easy to think of transitions or bridges to spiritual topics.

For instance, consider the following examples. "The weather sure does change a lot. Sometimes I think that my opinions about life and God are as changeable and uncertain as the weather. Do you ever feel that way? Most people do not know that the Bible has some very interesting things to say about the weather, especially as the time gets closer for Jesus to return to this earth." (Make sure that *you* know what the Bible has to say about the weather. Look up words in your concordance such as *wind, clouds, storm,* and so on.) "What—or who—ultimately determines the weather? Why can't we control the weather? (Probably because some lunatic would use this power to try taking over the world!) Has any person ever been able to control the weather (Mark 4:41)? What else could this person do?"

Health

Many Westerners are extremely health conscious, so you should have little trouble talking about this subject. Following are some bridges.

"Why are so many people concerned with their health? We all die anyway. Why don't people spend more time thinking about life after death, because that life will last a lot longer than this one? Which do you think should be more important, seventy years of good health on this earth or an eternity with God in heaven after this life? Is it a sin to overeat? The Bible tells us that God disapproves strongly when we harm our bodies. At the same time, He tells us that if we make it into heaven to be with Him, He is going to give us new bodies. If our bodies are a gift from God, should we be more concerned about the gift or the Giver? Which would make the Giver happier?"

Death

The subject of health can lead naturally into the topic of death. "Everyone dies. Is there no way out of this predicament? If not, are we concerned about life after death? The only reliable source on the subject of life after death would have to be someone who had actually died (not someone who suffered merely a short coma) and come back from the dead to tell us all about what 'the other side' was like. Has anyone done this? The foundation stone of true Christianity rests on the physical resurrection of Jesus. Do you think that there might be some truth to the Bible's account of Jesus' resurrection? Even if it sounds impossible, what if it were true? Would most people listen to Jesus? What if it were not true? How would that change Christianity today?

"A lot of people die young. How do you know if you will get old before you die? If you want to wait until the last minute to prepare for death, how do you know when that last minute will be? What if you are one minute late? Death comes to the young as well as to the old."

This is not necessarily a topic to discuss when your friend is grieving for a loved one who has recently died. You must remain sensitive to your friend's feelings. Make yourself available to listen and comfort your friend at the funeral or afterwards. The Lord may give you an opportunity to discuss what He has done on the cross and through His resurrection to overcome death.

Philosophy and Religion

Many people enjoy discussing religion, and once you are on the subject, it's an easy step to ask your friends if they have read the Bible and if they would like to do so with you over coffee once a week. If you have the time, after reading the Bible, read some other viewpoints on life, such as the Koran, Buddhist and Eastern religious philosophy, and so on. It would be helpful to read *The Universe Next Door*[1] or *Christian Apologetics in a World Community*.[2] These books will give you a good logical and biblical evaluation of many worldviews.

In my experience, religion, politics, money, and sex have been the topics about which most people get upset. Keep in mind that some people might *need* to be upset to drag them out of their mental lethargy. In some situations, you might need to pray for bravery on your part. You're not alone; the apostle Paul asked for such prayers for himself (Eph. 6:19).

Remember: Think through your possible conversations *beforehand* as much as possible. The possibilities are endless. You will gain confidence, and bridge-building will become easier the more you do it. I do not believe that this ability is a gift, because it has been learned by different people with different personalities. *It is simply a matter of practice.* Eventually, you might even find yourself looking for different bridges; the old ones have become boring! When this happens, do not fail to recognize the joy that you have begun to experience in your witnessing.

DO IT!

1. Pick one topic of discussion about which you feel comfortable talking. Pick one person with whom you would like to talk, using this topic of conversation. Plan a time to get together with him or her, over coffee or tea, at lunch break, or during an evening. Make it as convenient as possible for your friend. Write out five questions you can ask during the conversation that will make your friend think about more than just the topic at hand.

2. Look at your five questions and ask yourself, "What answers or objections will my friend give?" Write out responses to these answers and objections. Keep this thinking process going until your mind screams at you, "I'm tired!" Call your friend and make the appointment.

3. Before your friend arrives, *pray* that the Lord will guide your thoughts and comments.

4. Role play. This is one of the most effective ways of training yourself to witness! If you have a Christian friend who wants to witness to his friends, get together with him and role play different witnessing situations. One of you can play the part of an unsaved person and come up with objections to reading the Bible, why the Bible is not to be trusted, why organized religions are bad, and so on (i.e., all of the objections your unsaved friends have made or might make. Brainstorm!). The other person then can try to think up *questions* to ask in response to these objections. Stay away from giving answers. Questions are better for making your friends think. *Do this as often as you can.*

Chapter 6

What Do I Say Now?

How to Motivate Our Friends to Read the Bible with Us

"How do I make my friends curious enough to want to read the Bible with me?"

I will answer this question by showing how I have done it. I have recorded two theoretical witnessing situations, which are condensed versions of conversations I have had in the past few years. Everything that is recorded in these two conversations was actually said, either by myself or by the unsaved person with whom I was talking, usually over coffee and cakes.

You may ask how I came up with all of the right comments at the right times. In one word: practice! I spent hours talking to myself. I used the ideas that you are now practicing from the last chapter. I imagined conversations with someone with whom I wanted to read the Bible. I thought of questions or comments that I could use to make a friend curious. Then I asked myself what answer he might give and came up with a suitable response to his answer. I even wrote down many of these imaginary conversations in an effort to remember some of the more "intelligent" things that had occurred to me.

From these real and practiced conversations, I began to see certain principles emerge whenever I raised someone's curiosity. I will point out these principles in the following chapter.

These conversations should not be used verbatim, as if the exact wording will lead someone to Christ. They are given merely as examples and nothing more. They are not meant to be used as a script, although familiarity with the contents will probably better prepare you for your own conversations. Adapt them to fit your personality and your own friends. Do not emphasize the exact words but rather the principles behind them.

You will notice some repetition, the reason for which is two-fold. First, there are only a limited number of excuses unbelievers can offer for not reading the Bible. Second, the goal of this method is always to convince them to read the Bible, not to blow them away with the whole gospel using the shotgun method. Remember Hebrews 4:12-13.

Please feel free to use any of these comments or answers for yourself as you speak with your friends about your beliefs. You will begin to find the style that fits you. I would welcome any comments from you, the reader, on either this book or your own experiences in personal evangelism. As long as we are on this side of heaven, we are all still learning.

Conversation with a Friend

Karl and I met in a German-English translation class. We got to know each other over coffee and apple strudel between classes—sometimes even missing a class because we were enjoying each other's company so much. We had talked about everything under the sun. He read a lot of philosophy but was studying business. The job prospects for a philosopher were nil. He loved languages, spoke several fluently, and teased me about being illiterate because I knew only English and German.

We were driving to his place for a between-class coffee break when I popped the question. "Karl, what would you say if someone said he knew God?"

"I'd say he was crazy," he replied with no hesitation.

"Karl, I know God," I said seriously.

"You're crazy!" he said, again with no hesitation.

"Am I really?" I looked at him as we came to a traffic light.

He stared at me for a few seconds before he spoke. "No, you aren't crazy. You have some weird ideas at times, but you're not crazy!" He tried to smile, unsure where the conversation was going.

I returned his smile. "Weird, yes; crazy—you know I'm not crazy. And I'm serious."

As we turned down the street to his apartment, he motioned for me to drive on past his place. "This needs further discussion. I'll show you a park where we can walk and talk."

No one had ever confronted him so directly on the subject, and his nervousness dictated an attack. "No one can claim to know God," he said. "It's all in your mind. There is no God."

"Karl, have you had all the experiences of every human being who has ever lived?"

"No," he replied slowly. "I've only had my own experiences."

"Correct. Then is it possible that God lies outside your experiences? You say there is no God, but what you really mean is that you don't know Him if He does exist, right? If I told you about a person in another city, whom you did not know, you would not assume that that person did not exist just because you didn't know that person."

"But with God, it's different. You can't see Him!"

"Does that mean He doesn't exist? No, it doesn't. And we're back to my original comment. I know God. He lies within my experiences."

"On what basis can you say that you know God?" he asked finally.

"Have you ever read the Bible?" I asked.

"I gave up religion in high school. The religion teachers and leaders of the church were all hypocrites, and I saw through them. They were just doing their 'job' and were not interested in people. I never could believe that they represented God."

"Religion has always been that way. Men have been killing each other in the name of religion and 'God' for thousands of years."

Karl looked at me sideways. "But you just said you know God, and you mentioned the Bible. You aren't getting religious are you?"

"I'm not sure what you mean by 'religious.'"

"You know, becoming a fanatic about God and everything."

"Why would you assume that I'm becoming a fanatic about God just because I've mentioned the Bible?" I asked. "If I mentioned the Koran, would you think that I'm becoming a Muslim?"

"No," he answered. "It's just that nobody reads the Bible today, except priests and weirdos."

I laughed with him and asked, "And which one am I?"

"I'm not sure," he answered with a grin, "I'll have to think about it."

"Let me know what you decide. I know I'm not a priest, but I would like to know if I'm weird or not." Our friendship was solid enough that we could laugh easily at each other. "Have you read the New Testament?" I asked.

"No," he replied. "I'm not a theologian."

"Why do you have to be a theologian to read the Bible?"

"The Bible is too complicated for a layman to understand. It takes years of study to be able to understand it."

"Spoken like a true theologian," I replied.

"What do you mean by that?" he asked, a bit irritated.

"Doesn't it make sense that the theologians want us laymen to believe that only theologians can understand the Bible? If every Tom, Dick, and Harry could read and understand the Bible for himself, the theologians would be out of a job!"

Karl snorted. "What have you got against theologians?"

"Karl, please don't think that I'm criticizing or rejecting theologians. It's just that I haven't found anybody who can give me an answer to my question: Why do I have to be a theologian to read the Bible? If you were a Baptist or a Methodist or belonged to any other denomination, I would still be asking you the same question."

"You understand everything you read in the Bible?" he asked.

"Of course not! But I'll let you in on a little secret. Since I've been reading the Bible, I've discovered two things. The first is that I don't understand everything I read, but the second is that I understand the most important things. Mark Twain once said that he didn't understand everything in the Bible, but that didn't bother him. Then he added that the things he did understand scared him to death."

Karl did not seem to know whether to laugh at my statement. He obviously did not know what was in the Bible, and it seemed to disturb him that someone would say that something in the Bible scared him. I decided to illustrate my point with an area of his studies.

"You have studied languages. Do you understand everything in your new language book the first time you read it?"

"With *my* brain?" he asked. "Are you kidding? I can barely squeeze past an exam with a C if I haven't studied the text a number of times."

I laughed with him. "Do you throw the language book away because you don't understand everything the first time you read it?" I shook my head. "Of course not, or you wouldn't still be studying languages. And yet that's how most people treat the Bible." I opened my New Testament and acted as though I was reading it. "They read a few verses, come across something they don't understand, close it—" I snapped it shut. "—and never touch it again. But they will claim that they have read it and that it is not understandable."

I paused to let those words sink in. Then I continued, "If people want to believe that they can't understand the Bible, that's their problem. I'm not the smartest person in the world, but I can understand it. And if you've got brains enough to study languages, you can understand the Bible as well."

He wrinkled his forehead. I saw a question coming. "Then why do people study theology? Don't you need it to come up with the right interpretation of the Bible?"

"If that were true, then, after years of theology, wouldn't everyone come up with the same beliefs?"

He chuckled. "They certainly haven't done that," he said. "That's the main reason why I gave up. They were always fighting about how many angels could sit on the head of a pin!" His humor eased the heaviness of our conversation.

"Well," I said, "if the theologians do not agree with one another within their own system of theology, then I assume that they are not infallible; they can make mistakes."

"Of course," he replied, "no one is perfect."

"Then I want to know how I can determine when they have made a mistake and when they are right. I can't ask *them;* they're always right! I believe that God gave me a brain to use, not to switch off when I start having thoughts about God." I said these last two sentences flippantly to match his humor. "I have found the Bible extremely interesting. It tells me why I should not believe someone just because he has studied theology. Even if the theologian were right, the only way we could know would be to read the Bible for ourselves."

Karl made the expected comment. "But how can anybody as intelligent as yourself take the Bible seriously? The Bible was only written by men, it's outdated, and we can't know if what happened two thousand years ago was really passed down to us accurately anyway." His smile of satisfaction betrayed his feeling of triumph.

"Karl, I'm disappointed in you. You have studied philosophy, languages, and business, and you are intelligent enough to study physics, if you wanted to. Do you consider yourself scientifically minded?"

He had expected me to admit defeat and was disconcerted to have to answer another question. "Yes, I don't trust anything I can't examine with my five senses."

"Exactly! I'll give you an example. Let's say that you wrote a book on light. Another student comes to you and asks for some information on light. You give him your book and tell him that he will find out all he needs to know in your book. He comes back a week later and throws the book in your wastebasket and says that the book is just your opinion, it's outdated, and the facts are inaccurate. What would you say to him?"

"I would probably be upset at his insolence and arrogance."

"Quite right! And if you asked him if he had read the book and he said no? You would think he had a screw loose."

His sly smile told me he understood what I was driving at.

"Karl, you admitted that you have not read the New Testament. Is it scientific thinking to reject a book as worthless, outdated, and inaccurate before you have even read it?" I didn't need his answer; we both knew it, so I continued. "And besides, the New Testament is incredibly interesting. Would you like to read it with me? I would appreciate your viewpoint on some of the things I've read."

"You present a very convincing argument, but I don't consider myself religious," he answered. "I don't even believe that God exists."

"What does religion have to do with God?" I asked.

He looked at me with a comical, puzzled expression. "All religions claim to represent God."

"Does that mean that all religions do represent God? Isn't it possible that God might not agree with all of these representations?" He made no reply but was obviously deep in thought.

"I'll give you an example," I continued. "Let's assume that I claimed to be one of your closest friends. One day, you are introduced to someone and he says, 'Oh, I know one of your closest friends.' You ask who that might be, and he says my name, Floyd. You look at him and say, 'I don't know any Floyd. Who is he?' If you don't know me, am I one of your closest friends?"

He said nothing but nodded his head, agreeing with me.

"So how do we know who really represents God?" I asked.

He laughed and said, "Ask God!"

"Right!"

He stopped laughing. "I knew you were crazy!"

"That's very possible, but I'm not so crazy as to believe the many Christian splinter groups. I'm far too skeptical to believe any of them. The key question we have to ask ourselves is how we know what God is really like. When we analyze the world's organized religions, the only two conclusions we can reach are that either God is just a mixture of everything and nothing or the religions are wrong."

"But the Bible is just another religious book, like all the other religious books," he said, dismissing the reliability of the Bible with a wave of his hand.

"Could be," I agreed, "but if you were going to study Islam or any other world religion—Buddhism, Hinduism, and so on—how would you go about it? Would you analyze the many different factions among the Arabs to determine which group was really from Allah? Each group claims to be the true followers of Islam. How would you find out which one was right?"

"I don't see any way. It's the same thing with our so-called Christianity."

"Exactly! What is the standard of truth on which these groups rest their claims?"

"Well, the Muslims have the Koran. The Christians have the Bible."

"And who are the original representatives of these religions?"

He thought for a minute. "You mean Muhammad and Jesus?"

"Right! All the Christians claim to follow Jesus, but how can we know if they really do?"

He gave me a smile, as if he realized that he had been guided into a trap. "The Bible."

"Have you read it?"

"No."

"Wouldn't it make sense to read it to find out what Jesus actually said about God and following Him?"

"But how do we know that the Bible correctly reports what Jesus said over two thousand years ago?"

"We could ask the same question about the Koran or any other religious book. The first step is to read—" I raised my voice "—the Bible, or any other religious book, before we judge it as unreliable."

"Why should I accept the Bible over any other book—the Koran, for instance?"

"You shouldn't, until you've compared them. Have you ever

compared the life and teachings of Jesus as found in the Bible with the life and teachings of Muhammad in the Koran?"

"Okay, I'm waiting for the punch line. What cult are you with that you're trying to drag me into?"

I laughed out loud. "Boy, are you in for some surprises! Yes, I've won your friendship, and now I'm going to rip off all of your money."

He laughed. "I don't have any money!"

I continued, "Okay, so I picked the wrong victim!"

"You can say that again!" he agreed.

"I'm not connected with any religious cult, but I would like to read the New Testament with you."

"You've read the Bible. Why don't you just tell me what it says," he stated.

"No, if you really want to know what the Bible teaches, you'll have to read it for yourself."

"Why? I trust you!"

"Then you're thicker than I thought! I can think of no good reason why you should believe what I have to say about the Bible. All the religions and cults will gladly tell you what to believe. If you don't want to think for yourself, then go into any one of the churches or cults and ask them to give you something to believe. They'll be happy to do so. I'm not going to do that to you."

He looked at me, somewhat surprised.

"You know what I find interesting?" I continued.

"What?"

"Most people believe, in some way or another, that God created the human being. At the same time, when they talk about God and belief, they assume that belief rejects reason. If that were the case, why did God give us a brain? I find that to be an interesting contradiction. Well, I'm not ready to give up my mind. God gave it to me to use."

He slowly nodded in agreement.

"Remember our talk about skepticism?"

He opened his eyes wide in surprise. "Yes, you told me that

you were the world's biggest skeptic and that trusting people was the quickest way to get hurt in this life."

I nodded in agreement. "I really am a skeptic, but I've also read the Bible and know what I've found. I would like to ask you to read the Bible with me, but under two conditions."

He was listening intently.

"First, that you don't believe anything I say. I didn't write the Bible, and no one will ever get to God through my beliefs. I openly admit that I could be wrong, and, if so, you would be really stupid to follow me. It doesn't matter what I believe; it only matters what the Bible says and whether it is true. So, condition number one: Don't believe what I have to say about the Bible."

"And the second condition?" he asked, interested.

"The second condition: I won't interpret the Bible for you. We'll read it together, and you can tell me what the Bible says."

"Well, that's a new one," Karl remarked. "All cult leaders I've ever heard about want to cram their views down your throat. But how do I know that you won't interpret it for me?"

"Only one way to find out," I said.

"Right," he said, rolling his eyes toward the sky. "We read together, and I'll see. But even if you let me interpret it for myself, how do I know if I have the right interpretation?"

I smiled. "Good question. Many people raise the objection that each person interprets the Bible the way he or she wants to. Isn't it interesting that we don't think that way about any other book? If we read Hemingway or Kafka together, we would both agree on the basic interpretation of what they wrote. We might disagree on the application or outworking of their writings, but that's something else. If people read the Bible like any other book, there wouldn't be all those so-called interpretations."

Karl slowly nodded. "What you're saying is that we will read the Bible to see what it *says,* and then I'll tell you what it means."

"Exactly!" I exclaimed, "And I think you're going to be in for a surprise."

"I don't suppose you want to tell me now, do you?" He smiled knowingly. He had already picked up on the fact that I do not normally answer such questions, at least not right away.

I shook my head and said, "No, but I will say that I've read the Bible, and I have found that it doesn't need to be interpreted—just read. If a person is honest with the text and doesn't read anything into it, then the Bible interprets itself. You'll see. We won't treat the Bible as if it had a halo around it, and if you open it wrong you get zapped by God."

He laughed and slapped me on the back.

"We'll just read it like any other book. We won't take any passages out of context, but we'll read one of the gospels from the beginning to end." I looked at him, waiting for a response.

"I'm probably just as crazy as you, but what you say makes sense."

"When do we start?"

❧ ❧

We started reading that day and continued to do so for a number of weeks. One day, I asked if his girlfriend, Brigitta, believed in God.

"She used to, but not any more," he answered.

"What changed her thinking?"

He hesitated a moment. I wasn't sure if he wanted to tell me. "She used to be a good Catholic, but when we started living together, she lost her faith. Probably because she loves me—and I love her—and I haven't ever seen the need for God. At least not until recently." He tapped the New Testament I had given him.

"Does she know that you are reading the Bible with a crazy American cultist?" I spoke ironically.

"Sure," he answered and laughed. "I told her all about you the first week we met in translation class. We are planning a trip to Canada this summer, and she was glad that I had found someone to speak English with for a few months before we leave."

I do not fall into such open doors every day. "Would she be interested in reading the Bible with you and me in English if she wants?"

"Yes, I think she would," he said with no hesitation.

"Why don't the two of you come over next week and—"

"We were just going to ask if you and Christine and your boys could come for lunch sometime this week."

When my wife and I met Brigitta that week, we discovered that her friendliness matched Karl's, and we immediately became good friends with her as well. Convincing her to read the Bible was not as easy as Karl had imagined, however. When I finally got around to talking about spiritual things, she showed a fear of the Bible, which we came to discover was a common obstacle shared by most of our unsaved friends. In the end, though, she trusted Karl's intellect to keep them from falling into some cult.

One of her first questions was why we felt that we could understand the Bible without a theology degree. I gave her a different answer than I had given Karl earlier. I used the following example to answer her question.

"If God wanted to communicate Himself to the human race, how do we imagine Him doing that? Is He sitting in heaven, looking down on humankind, shaking His head in disgust at our stupidity and brainlessness? Has He decided to pick out a few of the smarter dummies from among us, whom we call theologians, to give us His information? Can you imagine God thinking, 'I'll just have to trust fate that those few educated dummies will get it right and pass along correctly what I say'?"

She laughed and told me that she had never thought about it.

"Is God really so incompetent and helpless?" I asked.

She shook her head.

"We may be more intelligent than the animals," I continued, "though sometimes I wonder, but the gap between us and God has to be millions of times greater than the gap between the animals and us. If God wanted to show us Himself, wouldn't He have to make it incredibly simple? Wouldn't He have to communicate in such a way that we could understand, assuming that we wanted to?"

She agreed.

"If an ant wanted to talk with me, what would he have to do?

He might walk over to me and talk to me in ant language, and I might understand him, but he certainly would not be able to understand me. First, I would have to want to communicate with the ant. We need to ask the same question about God. Does He even want to tell us about Himself? Why should He? Are we 'worthy' of this knowledge?

"Second, I would have to communicate with the ant in a language he could understand. The best idea would be to become an ant. But what if the other ants don't like me? What if they crucify—I mean kill—me? I'm not sure I would like that."

I tried to make this illustration sound funny, and she gained enough confidence in her own intellectual abilities to understand the Bible that she decided to read with us.

After a few weeks of reading together, they began to read other parts of the New Testament on their own. Shortly thereafter, they both came to realize that they did not need to rely on me as their "answer man." They were beginning to understand the Bible without depending on my questions, which originally had been meant to help them think. A year and a half later, they accepted Christ as their Savior.

DO IT!

1. Imagine the joy of having this kind of conversation with one of your own friends!
2. Reread this chapter along with the next chapter.

Chapter 7

The Principles of Witnessing to a Friend

It's Showtime!

I will use the "Conversation with a Friend" in the preceding chapter to illustrate ten principles of evangelism. Most of these principles can be applied every time you speak with an unsaved friend. Proficiency in witnessing comes from learning these principles and thinking about how you can incorporate them into your own talks (i.e., practicing imaginary conversations between yourself and your friends). The more you talk to yourself, the easier it gets!

> ### *PRINCIPLE 1:*
> **Become a friend before you become a preacher.**

Karl and I had been friends for a few weeks before I approached the subject of God. Some friendships open up faster than others. It usually depends on the freedom you feel to talk about spiritual things and on your friend's openness. There is no rule or set time limit. Each relationship will be different. In any case, our unsaved friends should recognize that we want to be their friends because we accept them as they are.

This might take a few days or a few months, but it is important that our friends see us reaching out to them as people, not as numbers to be added to our church rolls. If we do not want our friends to reject us automatically when we talk to them about the Bible, then we need to have laid a good foundation of trust. This trust will make it difficult for them to drop us as a friend, even if they find that the Lord is a stumbling block to them.

This principle applies to your neighbors, relatives you see regularly, work colleagues, and fellow students with whom you attend classes. This principle obviously does not apply to people with whom you do not have regular contact, such as people on the bus or train, people you meet on holiday or business trips, and so on. Two other principles for short-term acquaintances will be covered in the next chapters.

PRINCIPLE 2:
Do not condemn your friend.

Through our Bible reading with Karl and Brigitta, Christine and I learned another very important lesson pertaining to friendships with unsaved people. Karl and his girlfriend had been brought up to honor their religion, but this meant simply the outward form of religion: that is, going to church, paying their church taxes, doing a good deed now and then, and not committing any major crimes against society. Their religion had nothing to do with either their philosophy of life or their private lives. How they chose to live morally did not matter, as long as they were not openly living in adultery. Fornication, however, was quite acceptable for a number of reasons.

First, everybody did it. Once a person moved away from home and either went to university or got a job, it was more or less expected that he or she would find a suitable partner with whom to live until they both determined that they were suited for one another. A trial period was not only the normal practice but also encouraged by many parents and priests. In their view, divorce was a major sin, but fornication, if done "in love," was not.

Then, between three and five years later, they would get married. During the time they lived together before the wedding, they would have one or two children. The Austrian government paid them more social housing allowance to live together unmarried, and the woman was given a substantial sum for having children out of wedlock. Also, the two of them received child support from the government through their parents as long as they were "children" under the age of twenty-six, meaning "not married." A couple would benefit financially by staying together but unmarried for a few years first.

Karl and his girlfriend fit this normal pattern. When we first met and I discovered the situation, I was shocked, but I tried not to express this shock. Instead, I began asking them questions, and I came to realize how "normal" they saw themselves. I also began to see how "abnormal" my biblical views were as opposed to the social and religious norms.

At this point, I decided that I could not fight their whole immoral system all at once; I would have to handle it a step at a time. I asked myself how Jesus reached immoral but "good, religious" people. I reread the gospel of John, and when I came to chapter 4, I had my answer. He made the Samaritan woman curious by first showing Himself friendly to her, and then pointing out her sin. The order of these approaches seemed important, so I decided to try it in our Bible study each week.

My whole emphasis centered on the person of Christ. During our first few sessions together, I must have asked the question a hundred times, "Who is this person, Jesus?"

When we came to John 1:29, I still did not point out their immoral lifestyle. I simply asked them the following questions. "What is *sin*?"

They answered, "Everybody defines sin according to their own viewpoint."

"Correct. Does God have a viewpoint of sin, and if He does, is His viewpoint different from the human viewpoint?"

They had never thought of that. They did not know.

"If God does have a viewpoint, should we consider His viewpoint more important than our own or anyone else's?"

"Yes, that makes logical sense," they concluded.

"Then there are two key questions with which we need to wrestle. First, where can we find God's viewpoint? Should we go to the government for God's viewpoint?" Here we discussed politics, and it took a long time before they stopped laughing about equating politicians with God's standards of righteousness.

"Should we go to church?" Now they became uneasy. They knew the churches were not always right, but they also knew that they had no way of evaluating the churches' ideas, except by their own views and feelings.

"If the Bible is from God, wouldn't it make sense to read it to find out God's standard of right and wrong?"

Agreed.

"There is a second question, however. What if we read the Bible and discover that we don't agree with God's viewpoint? What if we discover that we, according to God's viewpoint, are living in sin?"

I did not tell them that they were living in sin. I did not say, "In my opinion, you are living in sin." My opinion would have been worthless at this time. Their whole culture spoke against my opinion, and there was absolutely no reason why they should accept my opinion, compared with everything they had been raised to believe.

After we finished John 4, then I could say, "The Bible teaches that it is sin for a man and a woman to live together and not be married." I still did not tell them my own opinion. At one point, they attacked me about this view, and I simply said that they would have to argue with Jesus about that. I did not write the Bible, and I did not tell Jesus what He had to accept as right and wrong. Then I asked them, "Do you have the right to tell Jesus what is right and wrong? If He is really God, as He claimed and demonstrated, doesn't He have the right to tell you how to live? I'm not going to tell you how to live! I'm not God. But what about Jesus? Is He God or isn't He?"

I have related this conversation to illustrate an important aspect of the friendship principle. When you start a friendship with someone who does not know the Lord, do not overreact to their sin. Do not condemn them on the spot for their immoral lifestyle. Let the Holy Spirit do that through their reading of God's Word. If you condemn them, you will be labeled a prude, and your friends will probably stop listening to you. It could spell the end of your verbal evangelism.

Some of our friends have stopped reading the Bible with us after the Holy Spirit convicted them of the sin in their lives. Although we were sad to see this reaction, we do not believe that we chased them off. We have come to expect some people to reject the conviction of the Holy Spirit. We keep the door of friendship open to them. We have not rejected them. They have stopped wanting to spend time with us.

Remember, the Lord Jesus could never have reached humankind if He had demanded a moral lifestyle before we were allowed to come to Him for forgiveness. He accepted people as they were and showed them the way to heaven.

If we have been brought up in a very moral climate, we might find spending time with immoral people difficult. We might feel that we will somehow be contaminated by them.

We must keep two things separate in our thinking: the sinner and the sin. The Lord Jesus loved the former and hated the latter.

We must accept our friends as they are before they will be willing to accept our message. Accept them as the Lord accepted you, and let the Holy Spirit, through their reading the Bible, condemn their sin.

Within a year, Karl and Brigitta began to see that if they wanted to consider themselves true Christians, real repentance required that they give up their immoral lifestyle by either separating or getting married. They chose to get married and are now becoming strong young leaders in a local church.

PRINCIPLE 3:
Take time to get to know them and use their felt needs as conversation starters.

When I first met Karl, I learned as much as possible about him by asking him questions about himself. I wanted to discover as much as I could about his personal life and his views on things.

This principle usually takes more time to carry out because friendship takes time to build, and people do not usually open up quickly.

Some people might be suffering from loneliness and others from an emptiness and lack of purpose in their lives. Someone might be struggling with a great lack of self-control in some moral area. Whatever area it is, the Bible has a remedy for their problem. Different needs require both different approaches and different answers. Everyone needs the Lord as his or her Savior, but the road to that decision might be different for each person.

PRINCIPLE 4:
Make others curious.

Through my conversations with Karl on various topics, I had begun to understand his analytical way of looking at things. Therefore I said, "I know God" because I knew he would want to know exactly what I meant. He thought that I was very arrogant, but this only spurred his curiosity more.

Curiosity can be sparked with a question or with a statement that your friend cannot understand. I will give further examples of conversation starters in a following chapter.

If you have trouble starting a conversation about the Bible, God, or religion, then provoke others to start the conversation. Be different! It doesn't have to be something wild, such as tattooing Jesus pictures on your forehead or breaking into a coughing fit when your friend lights a cigarette and then announcing that you don't smoke because you're a Christian. As I said in chapter 5, reading your Bible in public is a natural way to make people curious.

PRINCIPLE 5:
Ask questions!

Use this fifth principle to find out things about your unsaved friends in the initial stages of friendship and to make them curious about the gospel later. Start practicing now to ask different types of questions.

Ask questions that cause a person to doubt his own views: "Where did you get your information? Are you sure you know what you are talking about?"

Ask questions that place their morals in doubt: "Why should I live like everyone else? Why can't I be faithful to one partner all of my life? Why should I take drugs just because everyone else does? Why should I cheat on tests or steal at work just because it's so often done? Don't I have the right to choose my own standards by which to live? Why should conformity to everyone else be important to me?"

Ask questions that have no "good" answer: "What's wrong with reading the Bible?"

The key to asking the right questions is to think about which ones you want to ask before the situation arises.

PRINCIPLE 6:
Do not defend yourself.

This principle is one of the hardest to learn. It goes against our very nature and can be carried out only if we think through possible conversations with our friends beforehand.

As we saw in John 2 and 3, Jesus never defended Himself. He aggressively attacked the Pharisees' false presuppositions, and

He was not very polite about it. He dealt more kindly with those who came to Him seeking. The belligerent people received a different kind of treatment.

When Karl asked if I was becoming religious, my initial reaction would have been to run from his attack or to defend my Bible reading. My feelings told me to put my Bible away and tell him, no, I wasn't becoming religious, and then change the subject as quickly as possible. Or I might have felt as though I could somehow defend "being religious" (whatever that meant).

We have to remember that the believer can admit that he does not know everything and that he makes mistakes. This does not mean that the Bible is wrong or that Jesus will stop being God because of our failures.

With Karl, I overcame my initial reaction to defend myself by following principle five: I asked him a question. If he had said, "Have you had this problem long?" I would have still gotten the point: He is attacking my reading the Bible. My response? A question: "What problem?" Now he has to explain his question, and the sting has been removed from his question.

I could have asked him questions that put him on the defensive and made him see that he had no answer to my question: "Why shouldn't I be religious? Aren't you? Why not? What does God think about your not being religious?" In any case, I have avoided defending myself.

When people ask you for a reason for the hope that is within you (1 Peter 3:15), either give it to them or tell them that you will gladly read the Bible with them so that they can find the answer to their questions for themselves. Then perhaps they can obtain the same hope. If they attack you, however, do not defend yourself. Instead, ask them a question! It is difficult to think up questions on the spot, and it is no fun to be caught speechless by an accuser. Therefore, plan some questions you can ask. You won't be able to come up with just the right questions every time, but the more you plan for different possibilities, the more you will improve.

PRINCIPLE 7:
Do not try to prove that the Bible is true or that your viewpoints are right.

At first, Karl did not believe that the Bible was inspired by God. The believer knows that the Bible is not just any religious book. Hebrews 4:12 makes clear that the Word of God changes lives, not by placing people in a religious system or under a set of religious rules or by making them wear a religious mask. It changes men and women from the inside out. The power to change lives comes from the Word, not from our commentary on it. We simply need to get them to read it for themselves and let the Lord do the convicting.

Hebrews 11:6 also tells us that if people desire to be accepted by God and to please Him, they must believe that God exists and that He rewards those who come to Him. This is a prerequisite, not a final step in the journey to God.

What most people overlook is that belief or unbelief do not alter the facts. If we are told that there will be an earthquake tomorrow where we are living, and we choose to disbelieve this information, our disbelief will not stop the earthquake from happening. We could possibly die as a consequence of our unbelief. If, on the other hand, we believe that there *will* be an earthquake tomorrow, but there are no facts or indications of a future quake, then we can believe as hard as we want without causing an earthquake. Belief without facts is blindness; ignoring the facts is stupid.

If the Bible is not God's Word, then our viewpoints aren't worth the air we use to express them. If the Bible is what it claims, then this world's unbelief will not change the fact of the Bible's truthfulness. Even if we could prove the Bible to be true, most people would still reject it.

Many people will try to put you on the spot and get themselves off the hook by demanding that you prove something. "Prove that God exists! Prove that the Bible is true!" Don't try to prove anything. Jesus never tried to prove God's existence or that the Bible was true. He assumed it.

I once asked a fellow to prove to me that God was not looking over this fellow's shoulder and laughing at his reasons for
claiming that God did not exist. Then I asked him if God might
not be angry at being rejected by my atheist friend. Note principle five: Ask questions.

If an unbeliever states that most people do not believe the Bible,
I would agree with him and then ask him if the majority is always
right. This question has led to some interesting conversations about
politics. (In one year, during the 1880s, the French changed govern-
ments seven times. Each time, the majority ruled. If the majority
was always right, they sure changed their minds a lot!)

In line with this thinking, I often ask the person, "On whose
side would you rather be: all of humankind's combined or God's?"
I do not usually receive an answer.

If my friend seems to have honest questions about the validity
or trustworthiness of the Bible, I direct him to F. F. Bruce's
book *New Testament Documents: Are They Reliable?*[1] or Josh
McDowell's *Evidence That Demands a Verdict*.[2] These questions are very important, and if he really wants answers, he will
read these books.

When Karl said that I must be a weirdo, I laughed. Why? Two
reasons: The conversation was going well but getting warm, so I
needed to lighten it up. I was not bothered by his insinuation
that there might be something wrong with my brain. Maybe
there is! Don't take yourself too seriously and don't take your
friends' negative comments too personally. Again, defensiveness
(remember principle six!) will bring the discussion to a halt, and
that defeats our purpose.

PRINCIPLE 8:
Show your friends that their thinking could be wrong.

I once asked Karl, "Is it possible that you could be wrong?
No one is perfect. No one thinks correctly about everything all

the time. And yet, each of us believes, or wants to believe, that our views on everything are correct, or we would change our views. Maybe the Bible is from God, and you've been thinking wrongly about it all along."

Let them know that you could be wrong, too; therefore, you are open to having your own ideas challenged. When they react negatively toward the Bible, ask them the question, "What is different about the Bible, as compared with other religious literature? If there is no difference, why do you have a negative attitude toward it?"

This principle is present in all of the conversations. To win people to Christ, we must show them that they have a wrong viewpoint about both God and themselves. Before they will recognize their sin for what it is, and thereby desire salvation from it, they must admit one simple fact—their thinking has been wrong. Use questions to point this out. Do not say to your friends, "Boy, are you stupid! That's one of the most idiotic statements I have ever heard!" Such comments are door-closers.

The first goal of witnessing deals directly with this principle. Read 2 Corinthians 10:3-5 and Jeremiah 1:10. We are in the business of destroying wrong thought patterns. Look again at chapter 3. Our friends need to begin questioning their own viewpoints. "How do I know I'm right?"

A major area of wrong thinking for our unsaved friends concerns their viewpoint of the Bible. I asked Karl if he had read the New Testament. This is a critical question. He had negative feelings about reading the Bible, but he was not aware that he did not feel this way about other religious books. If the Bible was just another religious book, why did he react so negatively against my reading it?

Most people do not realize that their negative attitudes toward the Bible are not based on direct, first-hand experience. An important step along the road to getting your friend to read the Bible with you is to point out to him that he might not really know what the Bible teaches. A lack of facts leads to wrong thinking, especially if he has not read it himself.

Theology and theologians may need to be discussed, too. I expressed my thoughts on theologians to make Karl ask the question, "Can I really trust what they say about the Bible? My friend claims that he can understand the Bible, and he doesn't sound like a theologian. Maybe I can understand it without a 'religious' person explaining it to me. Maybe not all of it at once, but surely as much as my friend."

If you *have* studied theology, the answer to Karl's question "Have you studied theology?" could be, "Why do I need theology to read the Bible?" Remember, always try to answer questions with questions. My own theology degree could be a great stumbling block to unbelievers, and I really *do* believe that a theology degree is completely *unnecessary* for understanding the Bible. If you've studied some theology and are trying to reach the unsaved, you might need to unlearn your theological jargon and learn to speak like a "normal person."

Karl also thought that he was being intellectually consistent in his thinking, but few unsaved people are. In destroying Karl's argument about being intellectual, I attacked what Karl felt was his strong point—a logical and scholarly mind. I accused him of not living up to his own standard of measurement as a student. If he chose to reject me, the question would forever nag at him: "How can I claim to be a scientific thinker and reject a book I have not even taken the trouble to examine?"

Most people confuse religion with the Bible, and because they do, they reject the Bible along with all of their bad religious experiences. Karl also reacted this way when I mentioned the Bible. Therefore, I spent some time pointing out his lack of logical thinking in this area. My agreeing with him in his attitude toward religion accomplished two things. It showed him not only that we were not far apart in our thinking but also that he did not yet fully understand my way of thinking. It helped to make him more curious.

Another point to make concerning the difference between religion and relationship can be seen in church history. There is no use denying that "religion" has been the cause of many of the world's problems. A large percentage of the crimes against society throughout the centuries have been committed in the name of religion. The Crusades and the Inquisition in the Middle Ages were carried out in the name of Christ. The followers of Islam have murdered thousands of people in the name of Allah. In John 16:1-3, Jesus says that anyone who kills a believer in the name of God does not know the real, living God. Jesus condemned the organized religions of His day. Your friend may be baffled to discover that you find "religion" as distasteful as he does. It will help to make him curious.

Because a person can think wrongly, and because there are so many false religions that lead away from the one true God, I believe that a person should be, in his very nature, skeptical. This surprises many of my unsaved friends because they expect me to be "brainless," blindly believing what I've been taught to believe. True Christianity is not anti-intellectual. Tell your friend, "You need to use your brain, not your feelings, when you read the Bible." The apostle Paul, with his tremendous education as a Pharisee, is an excellent example of this fact.

Throughout the conversation, I did not accuse Karl in an unfriendly way. In the course of our discussion, I remained courteous but confident in my line of reasoning. One of my last comments to Karl was that the Bible was interesting. By then, I knew he probably would not ask "why" the Bible is interesting, but he would most certainly wonder what I meant.

Although there are more areas, these are the main ones with which you might have to deal in revealing to your friend his wrong thinking: a negative attitude toward the Bible but not toward other religious books, rejection of the Bible without having read it, trust in theologians who might be wrong, double intellectual (or emotional!) standards, and confusion of religion with relationship.

How does one go about showing an unsaved friend that his thinking is wrong? In chapter 3, we told of a man who owns a piece of land on which an old house stands. It would be difficult for him to build a second house on the land with the first house still standing. He would have to remove the old house first.

What is the fastest way to bring down an old house? Simple. Take out a few of the foundation stones, and the house will collapse. We don't need to use a cannon or a machine-gun approach on our friends. We just need to find a person's foundation stones and, with a few unsettling questions, remove them.

PRINCIPLE 9:
Do not answer all of your friend's questions and do not give him answers.

Stated another way, do not become the authority figure, the one with the right belief. Make the Bible central.

Throughout our time of talking about God, religion, and the Bible, and reading the New Testament together, I refrained from answering most of Karl's questions. He got angry a couple of times, but I kept insisting that what *I* believed was not important. If there was a heaven, *my* beliefs would not get *him* into it. He would have to find his own answers.

Make your friend come up with his own answers from the text itself. This principle applies both now and when you start reading the Bible together. It is vitally important that you establish the Bible as the final authority. Your opinion of the Bible does not matter. We will see this in action in the commentary section of this book.

I let Karl know that I did not consider myself infallible. I wanted him to see me as I am—just human, like himself. I can make mistakes, but I'm not afraid to admit it. I will always have something to learn from him, even when I see things correctly and he doesn't. And whether *I* am right or wrong will make no difference in *his* relationship with the living God. That all depends on whether *his* thinking is right or wrong.

At the same time, I challenged his claim that there is no God. I forced him to question his own "infallibility." His views were based on his limited experience. He had neither met a real Christian nor read the Bible seriously. He, like most people, never questioned his presuppositions and automatically assumed that his views on everything were correct. I had to deal with Karl's nonthinking attitudes at the outset.

PRINCIPLE 10:
Ask your unsaved friend if he would like to read the Bible with you.

Finally, principles one through nine should lead you to the ultimate goal of getting your unsaved friend to read the Bible with you. The Lord Jesus placed the highest priority on God's Word, commanding the Sadducees to spend more time studying the Scriptures (John 5:39).

If he says no, ask him why not, and continue the conversation. If his "no!" is final, keep the door of friendship open to him but find someone else to ask to read John's gospel with you. The key is perseverance. Don't give up!

DO IT!

Think back on a couple of previous witnessing experiences. Answer the following questions.

1. Had I been praying for my friend before I witnessed to him? Did the person I witnessed to believe that I was his friend? Did I get too personal too quickly? Was I close enough to him to know his needs? Did I show him acceptance before talking about his sin? Can I start over with this person? ("I'm sorry, friend. I didn't mean to hurt you with what I said.")
2. Did I make him curious, or did I unload the whole gospel at once? How could I have improved my approach?
3. Did I ask questions, or did I tell him the answers? Did he know and understand the questions behind my answers?

4. When he came back with his own questions, did I admit my failings, or did I defend myself? Did I try to meet his demands by proving something? Can I go back to him and say, "Friend, could we read the Bible together and then talk about proving things?"

5. Was I able to point out his wrong thinking without condemning him personally?

6. Did I try to answer all of his questions? If so, did he reject my answers because they were "my" answers?

7. Could I go to him now and ask him if he would like to read the Bible with me? If he says "no," can I ask why not and then use the principles in this chapter to help him change his mind?

8. If all else fails, can I ask another friend to read the Bible with me?

Chapter 8

A Conversation with a Stranger

It's Easier than It Looks!

Witnessing to a stranger allows you to do more talking, instead of just asking questions. Because you might never see this person again, you can choose either to make him incredibly curious or to give him as much information as you think he can handle at one time. In the following witnessing situation, I chose to do both.

I went sailing on a regatta once with some unsaved people because I wanted to improve my sailing. I did not know these people, but I knew that they would not be interested in talking about spiritual things, just about sailing. Therefore, although I had prayed all through the regatta for an opportunity to talk to any one of the crew about the Lord, I had set my witnessing antenna on low and had not expected to see God open the door. On the sail home, He taught me an important principle about witnessing to strangers.

꙰   ꙰

The moon shone full on the mainsail as a light wind blew us forward on our course. We had not won the regatta, but we had gained valuable experience for the next race, and we had become good friends during the four days of competitive sailing. The winners' party had lasted until eleven at night, but we had not slept afterward. Some of our crew had to be home by noon the next day, so we were heading back to home port on a six-hour night sail. Although Wolfgang and I had the first watch between midnight and two in the morning, Gerhard, our philosopher, and Max, our naturalist, were enjoying the ride on the open sea. Wolfgang was at the wheel.

The conversation started when Wolfgang related a story about a ship that went down under the Bora. The Bora is a violent, cold wind that comes off the Russian mountains, sweeps across the high, rugged Yugoslavian countryside, and drops suddenly on the unsuspecting boats that bob like corks off the coast. When the Bora hits, people die. I moved the conversation toward the subject of sudden death and discovered that Wolfgang had a great fear of death. The others listened silently.

"No one wants to die," I said, "but we all die sooner or later. We spend all our time trying to stay alive just a little bit longer, or we worry about how we are going to die. It seems to me that we are asking the wrong questions."

I paused to let them wonder which questions they *should* ask. They were not yet curious enough.

"We live only for an average of seventy years, and then we're dead for eternity. Why don't we ever ask the question, 'What happens to us after we die?'"

Wolfgang answered, "No one can know that."

"Unless someone died and came back from the dead to tell us about it," I said.

Wolfgang answered that some people have died "clinically" on the operating table.

I objected, "And maybe some of them had an experience of seeing a bright light at the end of a tunnel, but none of them were dead for more than a few seconds or a minute or two. I mean someone who had been dead for a day or more."

Gerhard could not contain himself any longer. "You don't mean Jesus Christ, do you?" he ridiculed.

"I didn't mention any names," I answered. "Did Jesus Christ rise from the dead?"

"Of course not!" Gerhard retorted.

"How do you know that?" I asked. "Were you around to inspect the grave?"

"You can't tell me you believe in the Resurrection," he said.

"Gerhard, it doesn't matter what I believe. If Jesus did not rise from the dead, then we can forget about Him, because He was just like all the rest of us. If He did rise from the dead, however, then we would be complete idiots not to listen to what He has to say about that experience."

Wolfgang nodded approval, but Gerhard answered, "The only testimony we have of Jesus is the Bible. You may be a good sailor, but you can't tell me that you believe the Bible! It's not trustworthy."

I allowed Gerhard to see the smile on my face, and he wrinkled his forehead, wondering what I found funny. Most people are alike. They raise questions as objections, claiming that the questions have no answers. They seem to think that the answers cannot exist because they don't know them.

"Gerhard, have you read the Bible?"

"No, I've been working on my doctorate in philosophy and haven't had the time."

"Then how do you know that the Bible is not trustworthy when you haven't even read it?"

"I read a verse somewhere once," Gerhard said, defending himself, "where Jesus said that the Christians have to drink blood. What do you have to say about that?" He obviously did not want to know the truth. He just wanted to put me on the defensive. So much for using the polite approach, I thought. If he is going to act like a Pharisee, then he should be treated like a Pharisee.

"You said you were working on your doctorate," I said.

He nodded.

"I assume you have to do research."

He nodded again.

"I wonder what your thesis is going to look like when you are finished. If you treat your sources like you treat the Bible, your thesis will be a jumble of run-together quotes, ripped out of their contexts, and stuck together to make everything say what you want it to say with no thought or concern for what the various authors really meant."

Gerhard's expression indicated that no one had ever returned his attack so blatantly.

"No one," I continued, "reads any kind of literature in the same way that you just misquoted a part of one verse out of the Bible. You pick up a book that you have never read before, open it to page 167, run your finger halfway down the page, pick out half of one sentence, misquote that half, and then claim that you can't understand the book! That is really intelligent. And you're working on your doctorate! Gerhard, I'm ashamed of you."

I had spoken these comments rapid-fire, and I made the last comment with the wave of my hand, indicating how useless I thought his doctorate would be under the above-mentioned conditions. Gerhard's face contorted in anger. Max got up and checked the jib to hide his embarrassment. Wolfgang had not noticed, or did not care about, Gerhard's feelings. He laughed.

"I've never been to college," Wolfgang said to me, "but I can see the logic in what you just said."

Max returned to his comfortable spot in the cockpit and exchanged glances with Gerhard.

"For me, God is in the stars," Max said, piously, as he looked up at the clear night heaven and waved his arm in a wide arc, indicating the millions of glittering stars overhead. "When I think of God, I think of the trees and nature." The finality in his voice communicated that here was a noble and permanent belief.

"That's an interesting way of looking at God," I said. "That viewpoint has been around for thousands of years. As far back as the Egyptians, we find people who believed that God was equal with nature.

"I have two problems with that, however. I can best explain what I mean by using an illustration. Let's say that I am a carpenter, which I'm not, and let's assume that one day I build a beautiful boat. You and a friend come along and see the boat, but I'm not home, so you see only the boat.

"When you see the boat, you make assumptions. You assume that somebody made the boat. You don't believe that it came into existence all by itself."

Max was listening intently. Maybe he really was seeking God, I thought, but too much pressure from Gerhard was keeping him from showing much outward interest.

"You are so impressed with the boat," I continued, "that you want to get to know the person who made it. As you start to leave, your friend says he wants to stay with the boat awhile. You leave and come back a few minutes later to find him talking to the boat. You ask him what he is doing, and he says, 'I'm getting to know the person who made this wonderful boat.' What would you think of your friend?"

Max could see what I was saying, but he was smiling, so I continued. "Granted, when I made the boat, I put a part of me into it, but no one would ever assume that I and the boat were identical. I am a living person, but that boat, as beautiful as it is, is just a dead boat. If you want to get to know me, you wouldn't talk to my boat. And if that dead boat is beautiful beyond description, then the living person who made it must be far more interesting that any of his creations.

"I don't understand how a person can look at those stars, their vastness, their order, their hidden mysteries that attract us to study them, and not want to find out what kind of a Being created them and put them out there."

A short silence followed, and then Wolfgang said, "Never looked at it that way before."

Max remained silent.

Gerhard's voice dripped with sarcasm. "Have you studied the stars?"

I smiled at him again—a smile can be very unsettling—and

spoke directly to him. "Stars give off light. Have you ever wondered what light is?"

No answer. They obviously had not studied physics.

"I spoke with a physics professor once and asked him if he could define light," I said. "He began by telling me that sometimes light acts like waves and sometimes like matter or particles. I interrupted him and said that I didn't want to know what light was like but what light *was*. He thought for a moment and then said, 'We don't know; we can only describe it.' I asked him if he had ever thought about God, and he said he had no interest in that area.

"Here was a man, who through his studies had received a small glimpse of the wonder of light, with all of its secrets. He was thoroughly fascinated by light and its intricacies. I was astounded. The possibility exists that there is a God who not only made light, but He thought up the idea 'light' and planned how light would work. This physicist couldn't even tell me what light is; he could just weakly describe some of its varied characteristics. And he did not have the slightest interest in the vastly more complicated God, who stands behind light."

I shook my head in disappointment and said, "To talk to the stars or to the sun is like talking to a boat or to a light bulb. What would you think of someone who spent his time talking to a light bulb?"

Max did not appear to be offended, while Wolfgang chuckled. Gerhard made no response.

I continued, "The other thing I don't understand is something that goes beyond mere knowledge or curiosity. All human beings have problems, and many people have problems for which they can find no solution. When a person is faced with such a problem and sees no way out, how can that person get comfort or help by talking to a star? To which tree should I go when my wife runs off with another man? To which star should I speak when my baby dies? How can nature answer my questions about death and suffering and pain? If nature is all there is, then these questions have no answers, and the entire history of the human race is one big accident. It becomes nobody's fault that thousands of people die yearly of hunger or cancer or AIDS."

I looked directly at Max, then asked rhetorically, "Is that satisfying to you? What good is an impersonal god? It makes more sense to believe in a personal God on whom we can blame everything!"

Gerhard was not to be moved. "Belief in a personal God is a crutch," he said. "Everyone believes that truth is relative. Every nation and people have different laws, and they are often applied arbitrarily. What evidence is there for an absolute God who gives out absolute truth?"

"If there is only relative truth, then my own laws are as good as anybody else's." I informed him.

"Right," Gerhard answered.

"And if, according to my law, I say that it is right to kill other people, then I have the right to do so within my law system."

"That's ridiculous!" Gerhard protested. "Society says that killing others is wrong."

"Which society?" I retorted. "And why should I listen to what society says? Different societies have different standards of what is right and wrong. Headhunters in South America don't think killing others is wrong. If all truth is relative, then those headhunters have just as much right to practice their beliefs as you do.

"If I believed that all truth was relative, then I could take your girlfriend for myself, regardless of whether you liked it or whether she liked it, and the only question left to ask would be, 'Who is stronger?' 'The survival of the fittest' becomes our final rule of life."

Wolfgang added, "When one looks at all of the wars into which we have gotten ourselves, it would seem that most people believe in this final rule."

Max nodded.

I continued, "But if there is a God, then everything depends on what kind of God He is. If He is only a superhuman God, like the Greeks imagined, then He is no different from people, just more dangerous. We don't talk about loving an arbitrary God; we only talk in whispers about fearing and appeasing Him. This kind of God will always 'survive' and win because He is the strongest. If God is absolute, however, then doesn't He have the right to set down His absolute law? He certainly has the power to enforce it!"

Gerhard's violent reaction broke the calm of the breeze blowing through the sails. "I totally reject such a God who can force me to do anything! I do not believe in such a being, and if He exists, then I want nothing to do with Him! I am free to do as I wish. I have a free will, and God is not going to dictate anything to me!"

"Gerhard, thank you for stating that so bluntly," I replied. "If you promise not to throw me overboard, I would like to point out two things you may have overlooked." I said this more as a question than a statement.

Gerhard realized how viciously he had spoken and laughed to cover up his reaction. "Sure, we're just having a discussion. It has no meaning," he said with a shrug.

"If I were to stand out on the main road at six o'clock on a Friday afternoon and say to myself, 'I don't believe that thousands of cars are going to run over me; I don't believe. . . .'" Smash! I slammed my hand down onto the deck hard.

All three men jumped and stared at me in surprise.

"It doesn't matter what I believe; I would be dead. My unbelief did not change the fact of those cars. Nor did my unbelief keep them from running over me.

"If there is a God, my choosing not to believe in Him will not make Him go away. Only children believe that they can wish something away."

Gerhard looked as though he wanted to throw me overboard. I judged the coastline to be about five miles away.

"And second," I continued, "you're right that every person has a free will to accept or reject God. Whether acceptance or rejection is good or bad, depends on the God that is accepted or rejected.

"I have no problem rejecting the idea of God as a hateful

being who hurts men for His own enjoyment. But let me picture another God for you. What if God is a God of love who sees me as I am with all my imperfections? And what if He accepts me as I am? What if He wants to communicate with me and becomes a human being to do so? What if He wants to make me better or even make me like Himself? What if He is willing to give me the entire universe? What if He is a perfect God and the only way to make me perfect is to die for me—to become a man and to give His life for me?"

I looked at each of them as I asked the next question. "Have you ever had anyone die for you? Imagine sitting on a railway line with a friend, and a train comes along. Your friend sees the train, but you don't. Your friend has just enough time to jump or push you. He chooses to push you, and he is spread over the next mile of track. What would you think of this friend?" I gave them a few moments to think about the illustration.

Gerhard looked thoughtful.

"You probably wouldn't forget him very quickly, would you?" I asked. "But we must not forget to ask another important question. What did your friend think of you? He considered your life worth more than his own.

"Would you go around claiming your friend did not exist? Would you tell everyone that he was an evil, wicked person? If you did, what kind of person would you be?

"Now imagine a God who loves you so much that He has done all these things for you. He has even gone so far as to send His Son to die on a cross, so you can go to heaven and live with Him forever. The only thing He requires of you is that you love Him in return. Have you ever thought about loving God?"

They clearly had not.

"I know," I said, raising both hands as if to ward off the obvious objection, "most people picture God sitting in heaven, looking down on humankind and thinking up all kinds of crazy laws, just to make life miserable. But what if God isn't like that? What if He wants to be loved by you and me? If He is a loving God, has given us His Son, wants to give us the universe, and wants us to live with Him in a love relationship forever, doesn't He have the right to be loved in return?"

Make the punch line good, I told myself.

"And then we choose to spit in His face and reject Him, all the time continuing to accept, without thanks, the very air we breathe. And with this air we breathe out threats and rejections toward Him."

I looked right at Gerhard as I said, "And we do it all in the name of intellect. Doesn't God have the right to get angry at our insolence and hard-heartedness?"

I began to wonder if I could swim the five miles to shore. Gerhard would have been delighted to feed me to the sharks, I thought. I had attacked his stronghold—his intellect—the unforgivable sin in academic circles. It was his turn.

"Most Christians I know act 'holier than thou,'" he said. "And they aren't any more intelligent than the average Joe on the street." He pointed at me as he made these comments. "They act like they are perfect and don't have any problems. If you ask me, I think they're all hypocrites."

I laughed out loud at this comment. "Gerhard, I haven't met a person in my whole life who wasn't a hypocrite in some area of his life, myself included! No true Christian would ever claim to be perfect."

Gerhard was speechless.

"Maybe all those people you know are not true Christians," I said, still chuckling. "If we read the Bible to find out how Jesus defines a Christian, we might discover that there aren't as many Christians around as we thought."

Gerhard's pride had been severely damaged but was still afloat. He wouldn't look at the other two men. I saw no softening in his glare. A true Pharisee to the end. His pride would eventually consume him completely. I had only a few minutes left to make one final attempt at helping him see himself as he really was—an empty shell hiding behind a mask of pious intellectualism.

We were nearing the port, and Gerhard wanted to have the last word. "That all sounds good, but isn't it all a bit simplistic?

Just believe and everything will be rosy! That is much too easy. It has to be harder than that!"

I was aware of the tremendous pressure Gerhard was under. He had no further arguments or questions to cast doubt onto what I had said, and Max and Wolfgang were beginning to see through his facade. The considerate thing to say would have been, "You may be right. Let's talk about that sometime." Gerhard needed something more direct.

"Gerhard, you may be right," I said. "But if you're not, then you've built your whole life on a foundation of sand—your own pride and intellect. And when you die, you'll stand before God naked and empty. You won't impress God with your doctorate degrees. When you tell Him to let you into His heaven, He'll say, 'Why should I? You never let me into your life on earth!'"

The harbor light had come into view. We would have to drop the sails in a minute or two. Time to close. "Take your pick, Gerhard," I said. "Waste your life on yourself or spend an eternity with the living God. If you choose to reject God, then enjoy as much of this life as you can. Eternity is a long time to regret it. Let me know what you decide. I'm interested in your decision."

The boat rounded the last beacon, and we started preparing the yacht for docking.

Gerhard and I eventually did meet for lunch once, and he began to read John's gospel with me. After three months of reading together, he broke off our lunch dates. At our last meeting, in a packed restaurant, he screamed at me, "It is not human to have a Lord!"

"Exactly!" I told him. "That's exactly what Jesus wants to be—your Lord. Nothing more and nothing less."

For several years afterward, I met with Wolfgang occasionally to talk about sailing and the Bible. He was always afraid to read it.

The Principles of Witnessing to a Stranger

A believer can use most of the ten principles when witnessing to strangers, but two more principles should be considered in this situation.

PRINCIPLE 11:
Be ready, at any time, to get involved in a conversation about your faith.

When you witness to a stranger, you do not have a lot of time and might never see the person again. Although you don't have the time to make friends, the principles of friendliness remain the same.

The Lord used Wolfgang's openness to show me that I should witness to him. To have kept quiet and talked just about sailing would have been the same as telling Him, "No, I've got something better to do today. You'll have to get someone else to do this job for you."

The Lord might want you to witness to someone at two in the morning, just to see if telling others about Him is a top priority in your thinking.

A state of readiness requires some preparation. Carry things with you that you can use to start a conversation. I often use books as a jumping-off point. Maybe you could use knitting and talk about the interweaving threads of life.

The next principle appeared at the beginning of the conversation. Wolfgang brought up the subject of death, and I used it as a springboard. I did not, however, mention God or anything religious at this point. I let Wolfgang and the others bring that up.

PRINCIPLE 12:
When you first open the conversation, do not mention God or the Bible unless they do.

Try to find something with which they can identify. Find common ground and do not be in a hurry to turn the conversation around. Get to know them a little by asking them questions about themselves and your common ground. Start looking for a connecting point between your common ground and something that could lead to talking about spiritual things. In this conversation, I used the subject of death.

The subject of death never leaves us. You can easily start a conversation about the many causes of death. Everyone is concerned about health. As you speak with someone about their or your health, you can throw in a one-liner, "It seems ridiculous. We spend our whole lives trying to stay healthy, and we die anyway!" Or, "There are so many books on how to stay healthy, and yet they don't keep us from dying. I wonder why no one has written a book on how to die?"

No matter how you start the conversation, these are the questions toward which you are working. "What happens to us after death? Is there life after death? How can we know? Has anyone ever died and come back to tell us about it? Why do we die? What started death?"

All of these questions lead to reading the Bible to find out what it has to say about the subject of death. Even though you might never see them again, you want to have planted a seed and dug away a bit of their false foundation.

A number of times on the boat, the conversation started to lag. The others would have gladly dropped the subject, but I felt I would not get another chance to make them as curious as possible in such a short time span. Therefore, I kept the conversation going by asking a question, making an observation, or giving an illustration of what had just been said. If you are witnessing to a stranger and you sense that he is getting bored or too uncomfortable, ask him a question or give an illustration to arouse his curiosity again. Questions make people think, and they will usually listen to an illustration if it is interesting. Plan your illustrations for different parts of the gospel ahead of time.

Many of the principles that you used with your friends can and should be used with strangers. Consider, for example, how the following principles can be used.

Principle 3. Look for a person's need to use as a conversation starter, as I used the subject of death with Wolfgang.

Principle 4. Making them curious is a must.

Principle 5. Ask a lot of questions!

Principles 6 and 7. Do not defend yourself and do not try to prove anything. You do not have enough time to cover all of the ground, even if you tried.

Principle 8. You will have accomplished a lot if you cause a stranger to doubt his own viewpoints.

You obviously cannot follow principle 1 (become their friend) because you do not have the time, and you might never see them again anyway. You might or might not want to follow principles 2 (do not condemn them) and 9 (do not answer their questions; let the Bible do that). These will depend on the situation.

If you sense that further contact might be possible, and if you sense an openness on the stranger's part, carry out principle 10. Ask, "Would you like to read the Bible with me?" You never know how the Lord is working in a person's heart. You might be surprised with a positive answer.

DO IT!

1. Think of something you can do to make a stranger ask you about your faith this week.
2. Think of one illustration you could use to make a stranger curious about your views of life or the Bible.

Chapter 9

A Summary of the Twelve Principles

For a quick review, let's boil down to their essence the principles discussed in more detail in the previous two chapters.

Witnessing to Friends

1. Become a friend before you become a preacher.

If you preach at people before winning their trust and friendship, they will probably label you as a self-righteous snob and will assume that you think yourself better than anyone else. If they have come to trust you first, however, they will know that you care about them.

2. Do not condemn your friend.

The Lord accepted us all as sinners before condemning our sin. Our friends do not need to "clean up their lives" before accepting the Lord. That is a "good works" philosophy.

3. Look for a need in the person to use as a starting point.

Most people do not feel a need for God, but they are hurting somewhere. Many times Jesus reached out and met people's physical needs (healing, feeding, listening) before He gave them the Good News. Using His method will show our unsaved friends that we care about them as people, rather than as numbers to be won for our church membership rolls.

4. Make others curious.

Say something that your friends cannot understand or that would not make sense from their frame of reference. Toss out a few casual comments about your faith, the Bible, God, or the world—anything that will cause them to ask, "What did you mean by that?"

5. Ask questions!

Asking questions makes our friends think. Giving answers usually stops the conversation, and our friends will often tell us that "our" answers are not for them. Asking questions will help us avoid using Christian clichés and Christian vocabulary.

6. Do not defend yourself.

Christians are not perfect, and we will have far more success in our witnessing when we admit our imperfections. We are not trying to draw people to ourselves (are we?) but to the Lord Jesus Christ. He needs no defense. He is perfect.

7. Do not try to prove that the Bible is true or that your viewpoints are right.

The Bible does not need to be proved true. It needs to be believed and obeyed. God can defend His Word far better than we can.

8. Show your friends that their thinking could be wrong!

You best do this by asking questions that point out their inconsistencies. If you do make a statement, simply state their wrong view as a fact; do not use an accusing tone. If they say that you could be wrong, agree with them! Then say that you should read the Bible—why not together?

9. Do not answer all of your friends' questions and do not give them answers.

Stated another way, do not become the authority figure, the one with the right belief. Make the Bible central.

Memorize Hebrews 4:12-13. Do not forget that the Holy Spirit is at work convicting your unsaved friends (John 16:8-11).

10. Ask your unsaved friends if they would like to read the Bible with you.

This is your final goal. If you can get your friends to read the Bible, the Holy Spirit will do the rest.

Witnessing to Strangers

11. When witnessing to strangers, be ready at any time to get involved in a conversation about your faith.

Practice imaginary conversations in numerous situations: at work, at school, in a car, on outings, or working at your hobby. Pray daily that the Lord will open your eyes to each specific opportunity.

12. When you first open the conversation, do not mention God or the Bible unless they do.

Let them know that you are a normal person with everyday interests. You can get excited about this world because God made it. You do not want to compartmentalize Christianity as spiritual and everything else as secular.

Chapter 10

Witnessing to a Cult Member

"We've just discovered that our neighbors belong to a cult! How do we witness to them?"

This discovery could occur on any street any day of the week in today's world. The cults have grown explosively. They have redefined Christian terminology, added a trace of Bible knowledge, and been encouraged by the fact that many Christians are easily confused by their heresies. True Christians must admit to themselves that they have been neglecting two foundational principles in their own personal evangelism.

Teaching

First, many believers seem to have lost the ability to defend rationally and intellectually the doctrines they hold to be true. Christians today have become too dependent on "clergy" to perform all the necessary chores of Christianity, and many Christians (or those who claim to be) go to church just to be entertained. Hedonism rules the day.

The most important item on the agenda, then, is to *know the gospel first*. Believers need to take 2 Timothy 2:15 much more seriously: "Be *diligent* to present yourself approved to God as a workman who does not need to be ashamed, *handling accurately the word of truth*." Believers need to know not only *what* they believe, but also *why* they believe what they do. It is a shame when a Christian has to run to the telephone to call an already overworked minister because the believer is confronted at his door by a couple of Jehovah's Witnesses or Mormons. A little consistent study of the Bible could give him all of the answers he needs and a tremendous sense of confidence in the Word and his ability to "refute those who contradict" (Titus 1:9). He might even be able to preach Christ (i.e., evangelize these cult members).

The story is told of the training program of the U.S. Treasury Department, in which they teach their agents to detect counterfeit money. The new agents are required to memorize what real money looks like before they are allowed to come in contact with false money. After weeks of handling and studying real money, they have no problem identifying counterfeit money.

The principle is the same in dealing with a cult member. The better you know the Scriptures, or at least the basic message of the gospel, the more easily and quickly you will be able to identify and combat a counterfeit.

Love

The second principle is love. Our love needs to go out in two directions: toward our own believers and toward the cult members. We have seen supposedly strong Christians fall victim to a cult because the cult offered them love and acceptance, whereas they had no close friends in their own evangelical congregation. True Christianity is a balance of both truth and love, not just one or the other.

The cults expect to be rejected by Christians. Many of the cults thrive on persecution. It feeds their ego to think that they are suffering for their faith. Most cultists believe that they have progressed beyond historic Christianity and have found the ultimate truth themselves. This belief reveals itself in their attitude of superiority and resentment when someone tries to share the gospel with them. They are often offended when a Christian tries to convert them. The cultists quite often see the evangelical Christian as their enemy. They have transferred their antagonism for the gospel to the messengers of the gospel, and they believe that any person who disagrees with their views is to be rejected. The typical believer reacts to this antagonism by becoming defensive, instead of disarming the cultist by putting him or her at ease. Being friendly under fire is not easy, but it is necessary to break down the psychological conditioning of the cultist.

Approach

Having arrived at ground zero (teaching and love are back in their proper place), the Christian now needs some pointers on how to approach an actual situation. The starting point is what Walter Martin in his book *The Kingdom of the Cults*[1] calls "common ground." When you start a conversation with a cultist, you must insist that you both agree on the same final authority. In the case of the Christian, this must be the inspired Word of God, the Bible. Allow *only* the Bible to be used in the discussion and not the cultist's own literature. If this is not done, you will simply end up in an argument and possibly lose the opportunity of further discussions with your friend.

Second, you (and only you) should open in prayer, in which you *preach the gospel* in your prayer for two or three minutes, quoting Scriptures on sin, the need for forgiveness, and the deity and work of Christ in salvation. Do not take the time to have a prayer meeting. Just get the Word of God into his or her mind through your prayer. It will not "return void" (Isa. 55:11).

Third, knowing the doctrines of every cult would be advantageous but hardly feasible. It is, however, helpful if the believer knows the basis of all cult doctrine. All of the cults are dependent on good works and self-sacrifice to get into their heaven. All of them are based on a form of self-salvation that requires people to deliver themselves from sin through their own human effort with God's help. The best defense against these false suppositions is a clear understanding of the biblical teaching of the person and work of Christ and His salvation. During the discussion, the Christian must *define* and *apply* the *historic* meanings of these terms to have an understandable conversation with a cultist. Otherwise, the Christian will always be frustrated that the cultist is saying the same words but meaning something entirely different. A well-trained cultist can easily twist Scripture by redefining the terms, reading something into the text, or coming up with a unique interpretation of a "proof text." The cultist can be disarmed by the Scriptures themselves.

A Special Note

When your cultist friend comes up with a surprise interpretation of a verse, the burden of proof that he is right rests on him, not on you. You are not obligated to "disprove" every false view that comes along. You must hold the cultist responsible for proving that his view is right—on the basis of Scripture. Cultists have learned to intimidate Christians by the line of reasoning that "if you can't disprove my view, then my view is correct." Jesus said in Matthew 24:4, "See to it that no one misleads you." Cultists almost always choose unclear verses in the Bible on which to base their doctrines. Just because you do not understand an unclear verse in the Bible does not mean that the cultist's view of that verse is correct. Ten different cults might each hold a view of a particular verse in the Bible, and they *all* could be wrong! Point out to your cultist friend that a person who is seeking the truth should never base his doctrine on unclear verses because there is a much higher chance of coming up with the wrong interpretation (as evidenced by the multitude of cults!). Second Peter 3:16 might come in handy at this point. The burden of proof rests on the cultist, not on the Christian.

This principle applies to so-called miracles as well. The Christian needs to give serious heed to the words of Jesus in these last days: "For false Christs and false prophets will arise and will show great signs and wonders, so as to mislead, if possible, even the elect" (Matt. 24:24).

Seven-Step Summary

1. Know the basics of Christianity well.
2. Show yourself to be friendly.

3. Preach the gospel by opening in prayer.
4. Determine your final authority as "common ground."
5. Define the biblical terms and make the cultist define his or her terms.
6. Apply the biblical terms to yourself and your friend.
7. Repeat steps 2 through 6 again and again.

DO IT!

1. Have you taken for granted the doctrines you have been taught but couldn't defend these doctrines if confronted by a cult member? Get a Bible concordance and look up every Scripture reference to each basic doctrine and write your own personal theology on the basics. The basics of the gospel can be found in 1 Corinthians 15:3-4: the deity of Christ, the substitutionary atonement of the cross, and His bodily resurrection from the grave.

2. Obtain a copy of Walter Martin's book *Kingdom of the Cults,* and read chapters 2, 3, and 19 closely. Then read the chapter that deals specifically with the cult with which your friend is involved. Other very good books that deal with specific cults are on the market, and some of them go into more intricate detail than does Martin's book. The average believer, however, has only limited time to read other books aside from the Bible, and if you read Martin's whole book, it is thorough enough to arm you against any cult of the day.

3. Start praying for your cultist friend.

4. Invite your friend to do something with you *as a friend,* not as an enemy. If the subject of religion comes up, don't spoil your time together now; instead, make an appointment to get together specifically for the purpose of "doing battle." In any case, keep your sense of humor alive and show your friend that you accept him or her as someone valuable who has been made in the image of God, regardless of what he or she believes.

Chapter 11

Short Conversations

Each believer will experience a different variety of witnessing situations, and each time unsaved friends will seem to come up with new objections or reasons for not reading the Bible. I have discovered, however, that the average, unsaved person is very limited in his or her thinking, and there are, in fact, only a limited number of objections that can be raised.

A few years ago, I took Christine, my wife, to one of my evangelistic Bible studies. We had just begun John's gospel, and she wanted to meet these new people. The evening went as planned, and everyone was excited about returning the next week—even those who had raised the most objections. On our way home, Christine asked me if I had programmed the people to ask the questions they had asked or to make the objections they had made. I laughed and asked what she meant.

"I was astounded," she exclaimed. "Every time you come home from an evangelistic Bible study, you always tell me what happened—that is, what questions were asked and what objections were made. Tonight I heard all of the same questions and objections, as if they had all been to one of your previous studies or had learned the lines to a play."

At that point, I began to count the number of different objections raised against the gospel or against reading the Bible. I was astonished to find so few! Although there will be many

variations, the basic categories of questions and objections remain few in number.

You will encounter three kinds of people in your witnessing:
the complacent, the antagonistic, and the sincere. The complacent ones, the largest group, are often morally good people, but
they are not concerned about spiritual things. The antagonistic
ones, usually in the minority, will want to trip you up and make
a fool of you. The Lord handled both of these types harshly,
using what one might call "Pharisee Treatment."

The sincere ones are truly seeking the Lord and will eagerly
accept what you have to say, although maybe with some skepticism. Jesus gave these people direct answers to their searching
questions.

The kind of person to whom you are witnessing will determine your approach. It might take a little time to discover a
person's attitude toward spiritual things, but once you do, try to
remember how the Lord dealt with that type of attitude. You
will have your best success in witnessing to them if you use
Jesus' approach.

I have written out the conversations I have had with many of
my unsaved friends. Some are written out in conversational form
to give you an idea of actual situations. Others are simply my
questions and comments, written out as if I were talking to
someone. Still others are lists of options you can use to steer the
topic toward spiritual things, depending on where the conversation started.

Most of these conversations are one-way and very concen-
trated. You will probably never use a complete conversation at
any one time. On the other hand, I have most certainly not
exhausted the subject in any given conversation. Feel free to use
any of this material in your own evangelistic conversations.
Whatever you do, do *not* read the whole chapter in one sitting.
Instead, read a section from this chapter and then try to imagine having your own conversation with an unsaved friend *before*
you read any further.

Sample Objections
God Is Not Important to Me

Once while I was sitting in an office, a man told me that he did not have time for God. I asked him what was most important to him in life—his job, his family, his money, or his career. The following conversation took place.

"Different things are important to me at different times," he answered.

"Have you ever tried to see things from another person's viewpoint?" I asked.

"Of course," he said. "You have to if you want to get along with people."

"Have you ever thought about seeing things from God's viewpoint?"

"No," he said without hesitating. "I've never had to get along with God." He chuckled at his own joke.

I continued, "Most people have an opinion about God, but it doesn't seem as if many people ask themselves the question, 'What does God think of me?'" His expression told me that this thought had never occurred to him either. I did not give him any time to think of or voice an objection.

"If there is a God," I said, "and He never dies, then God's life goes on after we die. We all have different ideas of what heaven will be like, and most people want to go to heaven as long as God is not there. They want heaven to be perfect and beautiful—for them—but they are not interested in the God who may be there. They want His gifts and all that He has to give, but they don't want Him."

The man was becoming visibly uncomfortable, but he had made the brash statement that God was not important to him, so I decided to pour on the guilt. I would probably never see him again. I wanted to be sure he saw things from God's viewpoint at least one time before he entered eternity.

"It's like a little child at Christmas," I continued, trying to put him at ease, as though he was having an enjoyable conversation with a good friend. "The child takes gifts from his father, but when the father says, 'Let's play together,' the child rejects the father, and says, 'I'll like you and play with you if you give me more things.'" I paused for a split-second, and then asked, "Do you have children?"

"Yes . . . ," he said slowly.

"And you probably feel that you have the right to be loved by them." I nodded vigorously, giving him no time to change the subject. "Doesn't God have the right to be loved by us? When we ask ourselves 'Is God important to me?' we need to realize that what we are really asking is 'Do I want God or just His gifts?' Like that little child.

"If God gives us the air to breathe, and we take the air every few seconds but we don't thank God for it, and we don't want anything to do with God, why should God want to let us breathe any more? What right do we have to demand of God that He let us breathe? And if He made us, doesn't He have the right to do with His own property as He pleases?" I could hear the door opening. I had just a few seconds for the *coup de grâce*. He stood up to leave.

"Have a nice day. And I hope your children love you more than most people love God."

He left speechless. Our paths have not yet crossed again. Maybe in heaven.

God Does Not Exist

I once mentioned casually to Roland, an acquaintance, that I believed in God. He reacted violently and screamed, "You're intolerant! Completely intolerant!" He jumped up and began pacing back and forth. "You believe in God. No one could ever have a reasonable conversation with you because you are so intolerant! Belief in God always leads to tyranny!"

Quietly I asked, "Roland, are you intolerant of me? Do you reject me because I believe in God? Don't I have the freedom to believe what I want so long as I don't force my belief on others? If you had the power to do so, would you forbid belief in God? Would you become a tyrant?"

He switched topics in an attempt to avoid answering my questions. "Why does God allow all the suffering in the world?"

"Roland, if God does not exist, how can He be responsible for all the evil and suffering in the world?"

The strain was beginning to show on Roland's face. "You may be very good at talking most people into believing in God, but you're not going to take me in," he shouted. "I deny the existence of God!"

It probably wasn't the right time to laugh, but I couldn't help myself. He had folded his arms across his chest, and his chin jutted out like a small child who refused to eat his spinach.

I chuckled and then said, "Roland, let's suppose that there is a tree standing in the middle of this room. You and I come into the room and I say, 'Roland, I deny the existence of this tree.'" I folded my arms in mimicry of his attitude. "What would you think of me? If we were good friends, you might ask me what I meant. You might ask me how I can deny the existence of something that really exists. It would be a ridiculous statement to make.

"If, however, there was no tree in the room, and I yelled at you, 'I deny the existence of a tree in this room,' you would look around the room and then ask me what I was talking about. You might say to me, 'Stop being absurd!' What reason can there be for denying the existence of something that doesn't exist? The only reason for an adamant denial of its existence would be an intense hatred for trees.

"Either God exists or He doesn't, but my denying His existence won't change the facts. If a person does not know God, then the most that person can say—and remain intellectually honest—is that he is not sure if God exists. If you continue to deny God's existence when you don't know if there is a God, then I have just one question for you. Do you hate God?"

He exploded. "Yes! Yes, I hate God! God demands obedience. He doesn't allow people to be free. I am my own god. I don't need God. And when I die, I will require that He stand before me and account for all the bad that has happened to me.

I will demand that He meet my standards! I will not allow God to take away my freedom."

We had arrived at his main problem, and I turned the conversation toward the concept of freedom.

≈   ≈

A different conversation started when my sailing friend Gerhard said, "I have no trouble believing in chance. It is just as possible that God does not exist as it is that He does."

"That's true," I answered. "Anyway, you used the right word when you said you 'believe' in chance. It doesn't matter which presupposition you choose—there is a God or there is no God—both of them are founded on faith.

"When a person looks at the universe," I said, "and asks the question 'Where did it all come from?' the weight of evidence is on the side of believing that God exists. Of course, a person who isn't searching for the truth doesn't have to ask the question. He can go blindly through life hoping that everything will turn out all right when he dies, although he might not know what he means by 'all right.'

"If God does exist, the only way we could learn about Him would be if He communicated with us. Would you like to read the Bible to discover what it has to say about God's existence and His desire to communicate with us?"

A Seeker

Loving books as I do, I spend a lot of time in the local library and have gotten to know the local librarian, Peter. Upon asking him what he did on his holidays, he replied, "I like to travel to Findhorn, Scotland. There's a place where people try to make contact with the spirit world."

"Why do you want to make contact with the spirit world?" I asked.

He smiled, obviously enjoying a chance to talk about his beliefs. "I consider myself a seeker," he replied.

I complimented him on his openness and then asked if he would be interested in some observations I have made in the few experiences I have had in my short lifetime. No one else was in the library at the time, so he pushed his work aside, and I jumped in.

"I believe there are basically only three kinds of people in the world," I started. "Some people don't want anything to do with God. They have no interest in anything beyond their five senses. They don't want to listen to people like you and me, who have had experiences beyond their narrow corridor of reality."

Peter nodded his eager agreement.

"The second kind of people *claim* to be searching for God, but when asked what kind of god they are looking for, it becomes clear that they only want a god that fits their view of life. They want a god they can manipulate. They certainly don't want a god who requires anything of them. Many of these people are willing to have a give-and-take relationship with their god. They will go to church once a week and do a few good deeds, they will attempt to be as good as their 'neighbor,' and they will choose which neighbor. In return, they expect their god to let them into heaven. These people require God to change and fit into their ideas of Him."

Peter nodded slower this time. He did not seem to like my description of people who claim to be seekers.

"The third kind of people seek God and are willing to change their view to find the real God. These people admit that they can make mistakes. With so many religions in the world, they know that these religions cannot all be right. So these people set a goal to find the one true, living God and to worship Him—as He is and for what He is." I paused, then added, "Have you come across any other types of people?"

"I haven't really thought about it much, actually," he said.

I did not know what his reaction would be to my comments, but I wanted to make something of more importance clear to him.

"If there are only three kinds of people in the world, what

kind of person do you think God is looking for?" I let this question register then added, "Pascal, the French philosopher and mathematician, once said that God reveals Himself to those who seek Him with their whole heart, and He hides Himself from those who don't. Don't you agree that God has the right to do this?"

A person who reads the gospel of John will discover in John 4:23 that God wants people who are seeking Him "in spirit and in truth."

Alone or Lonely

Barbara, an unsaved student, had everything the world had to offer: physical beauty, financial security, intelligence, and dozens of friends. At lunch one day with my wife and me, she asked me if I could handle being alone. She did not want to know if I liked being alone but if I could cope with it.

I told her, yes, I could cope with it.

She shuddered and said, "I can't. My biggest fear is of being alone."

I said, "Barbara, you need to understand that when I'm alone, I'm never *alone*. There's a big difference between being alone and being lonely. A person can be alone but doesn't have to be lonely—if that person has a personal relationship with Jesus.

"On the other hand, a person can have many friends around her and always be going to parties as the most prominent social butterfly and be lonely. A person who has only herself with whom to talk, in whom to confide, and on whom to rely in time of need, in spite of all her friends, is to be pitied. That person needs a loving God, who can sweep away her loneliness like the dead, dry leaves of autumn and replace them with the fullness of spring sunshine."

What Is a Christian?

"Some people think that most people believe in Jesus and are, therefore, Christians. What is a Christian? Are you a Christian? I didn't ask you to what denomination or religion you belong. You could tell me that you came from Mars or had green skin, but are you a Christian?" (The point of this question is not to find out to which specific religion he belongs. That is not important. What we want to do is to get him to define what a Christian is.)

"How would you define a Christian? Do I have to belong to a specific denomination to consider myself a Christian? Why do you consider the people in your denomination Christians? What makes them Christians? How did they become Christians? If everyone who goes to a Catholic or Protestant church is a Christian, then being in a particular church does not make you a Christian. Being born in America or Austria or any other country doesn't make a person a Christian. There are atheists in every country. There must be some criteria that determine what a Christian is.

"We could ask the same question about the followers of any other religion. What is a Buddhist? We could go to Buddha and ask him what a Buddhist is. He would probably say, 'Someone who accepts the teaching of the Buddha and follows those teachings.' What is a Muslim? We would go to Muhammad and ask him what a Muslim is. He would probably say, 'Someone who accepts and follows the writings of Mohammad.' How do we know what a Christian is?

"Isn't a Christian someone who follows the teachings of Christ? If we went to Jesus and asked Him, would He say that we were Christians?" (Most people will have no answer for this question. They have never thought about Jesus' viewpoint on anything.)

"I might tell myself that I am a Christian, or a specific church or government or family member might tell me that I'm a Christian, but what would Jesus say? The word *Christian* means 'someone who follows Christ.' What if I believed that I was a Christian, but when I died, Jesus said that He didn't know that I was a Christian?

"Does a person have to be perfect to be a Christian? On the one hand, we look around at those claiming to be Christians, and we say, 'They can't be true Christians because they don't act like Christians.' On the other hand, we admit that nobody is perfect, not even a Christian, whatever that is. If a person has to be perfect to be a Christian, then there can't be any Christians! I could say that some people are better Christians than others, but that still doesn't answer the question, 'What is a Christian?'

"The best way to find out what a Christian is, is to read the New Testament and find out what Jesus says about that. As for Christians being better than others, that is obviously wrong. There is a basic difference, however, between a Christian and a non-Christian. I'll give you an example.

"Let's suppose that we are both beggars. Beggars have to search constantly for their food, and sometimes they share their food with another beggar. One day, I come to you and I say, 'I know where some bread is. Come with me and you can have some too.'

"You look at me skeptically and say, 'I don't believe you.' I say, 'I don't care if you believe me or not. The fact is that I know where some bread is, and if you want some, you're going to have to come and get it. The least you can do is come and see if I'm telling the truth.'

"To which you reply, 'Oh, you just think that you're better than the rest of us.'

"My answer to that is quite simple. 'No, I'm not better than you, but because I know where some bread is, I am certainly *better off* than you. You have to decide if you want to be in my position and have bread as I do.'

"Christians are not better than other people. But if there is a God, and if these Christians know Him, and if God has told them that He will gladly take them to heaven just because they believe in Him and accept Him [pause to take a breath], then these Christians are most certainly better off than other people, who don't have such an assurance!

"Would you like to read the Bible with me to see how Jesus defines a Christian? Would you like to read the Bible with me to learn how to become a Christian?"

What Is the Difference Between a Christian and a Non-Christian?

Someone might say, "I don't see any difference between you and me. We both have problems."

You can respond, "That's correct, we both have problems. If any Christian ever says that because he has become a Christian he doesn't have any more problems, then he probably isn't a Christian. Jesus tells us that the Christian is a foreigner in this world and that the Devil hates him. How would you like to be on someone's hate list? The more you are committed to Jesus, the higher you are on the list."

"I still say that Christianity is a crutch for weak people," comes the reply.

"Could be. Let's compare you, a non-Christian, with a Christian. No one has a problem-free life. You face tremendous problems and pressures in your work, in your family, and among your friends. Everyone has been let down or betrayed by a friend at one time or another. You have to solve all of the problems alone. You can't turn to God because you don't have a personal relationship with God. You can only hope that God, whoever He is, will stoop down and help you out somehow. You are not even sure that you don't have a problem with God Himself! When you ask the question, 'What does God think about my sin?' you don't have an answer. If you ask, 'If I die tonight, am I sure that I will go to heaven?' you don't have an answer for that either. You have plenty of problems in this life, and in addition, you don't know whether or not you're going to have far worse problems in the next life!

"Then we look at a Christian. He has all the same problems, plus some additional ones. He will be rejected by some of his family. He will be laughed at for his belief. Those who hate him for his belief will discriminate against him. If he takes his faith seriously, he will be in the minority and have only a few true friends. We could almost say he must be crazy to have made the decision to become a Christian!

"However, there are some problems he no longer has. He

now has a personal relationship with the living God, and he knows where he is going after he dies. He no longer has any problem with God; on the contrary, God is always there helping him through his problems in this life!

"Most of the problems we have concern our relationships with other people. Neither the non-Christian nor the Christian has peace with all other people. Only the Christian can say, 'I have peace with God.' Only the Christian can say, 'What God thinks of me is more important that what others think of me.'

"What would you rather have—problems with other people and with God or problems just with other people and peace with God?"

Good Deeds (God's Standards for Entering Heaven)

"Some people believe that if they work hard, do good deeds, and are good enough, they will get into heaven. How hard is hard enough? If you try to keep the Ten Commandments and are as good as the next guy, will God let you into heaven? What if God doesn't let the 'next guy' into heaven? When you say that you're good enough, aren't you measuring yourself against a relative standard? Have you ever asked yourself what God's standard is for letting us into heaven?" (Most people have nothing to say to these questions. They have never given any thought to God's viewpoint on the subject. They have assumed that their viewpoint is correct. We want to help them see things from God's perspective.)

"Do we really believe that we can come to God on our own terms? Doesn't heaven belong to God? Doesn't He have the right to decide whom He wants to let in? What kind of person believes that he can dictate to God his terms of acceptance into heaven? If there is a judgment at the end of all time, will you judge God or will He judge you? If you were a teacher, would you let the students make up the exams and determine their own grades? What would you say to a student who does very poorly on an exam then demands to be given a higher grade just because he thinks that you grade too hard? What will God say to those who demand that He accept them on their own terms?" (These questions will unsettle most people. If an unbeliever has a haughty attitude toward God, these questions will normally force that person to see the foolishness of such an attitude.)

"If you died right now and you stood before the gates of heaven, what would you say to God if He asked you, 'So who are you? Why should I let you into my heaven?' Would you point to your good deeds? What if God wanted to know why you felt you were good enough to be allowed into heaven? What would you answer? Is it possible to know God's standard? How?" (Be careful how you answer this question. An outright statement that the Bible is from God could end the conversation.)

"Let's answer those questions with a couple of additional questions. Is everything in heaven perfect? Most people will reply, 'Of course.' Are we perfect? Of course not. Even though we have difficulty imagining what perfection is like, we still know that we are not perfect. If we are not perfect, however, and you or I died and went to heaven, then heaven wouldn't be perfect any more! Why should God let imperfect beings into His heaven? The conclusion is that nobody can get into heaven! Nobody is perfect!

"If going to heaven depended on meeting God's standard of perfection, then no one could make it. And to make things even worse, God tells us in the Bible, in James 2:10, that if we break just one of God's laws, then we are guilty of breaking the whole law.

"And yet, I know that I'm going to heaven." (This last comment always draws a sharp reaction.) "No, I am not saying that I am perfect. Quite the contrary! I'm no better that anyone else, and in some cases I'm worse than some people. Anybody who thinks that I'm perfect needs only to talk to my wife. She knows that I'm not perfect!" (At this point in the conversation, I usually give the illustration of the two beggars. This illustration is given under the earlier short conversation, "What is a Christian?" After the illustration, I add, "No, I'm not going to heaven because I'm better than anyone else, and I'm certainly not perfect. I'm going to heaven for another reason." I usually say no more. If this illustration and my last comment do not make my friend curious, then nothing will.)

"Some people hope that God will act like a loving grandfather, that He will simply close an eye to their wrongdoings and let them into heaven anyway. If God did that, however, then He would not be righteous. People want a God who gives others what they deserve but who closes an eye when it's their turn. If God acted this way, then no one could be sure how God would react when each one of us faces Him in the end. God has to remain fair and treat everyone alike.

"Others object by saying that a loving God will not judge us at all. Can you imagine listening to the news one day and hearing that the president has closed all of the prisons and released all of the murderers and rapists, giving them all pardons? When someone asked him why he did such a thing, he replied, 'We should be more like God and love these people; therefore, I let them all go free without any punishment.'

"Do you know what that would mean? People could murder each other, knowing that no one would be punished. Anarchy would reign and human life would become worthless. We do not want our government to run that way. Why do we expect God to define *love* in that way? Won't God be even more righteous than our court system? God has to judge each one of us to remain fair and impartial.

"Someone might say, 'That all sounds good, but isn't it all a bit simplistic? Just believe, and everything will be rosy! That is much too easy. It has to be harder than that!' So you think that because we are a people of progress, the biblical way to heaven is too simple. It's too difficult for educated people to accept such a simple belief. If this belief is too simple, then how hard do you want to make it? Let's say that if you do *only* good deeds for one hundred years, then you will be allowed into God's heaven. How does that sound?

"You might say, 'But none of us will live another hundred years!' Oh, I'm sorry, I hadn't thought of that. Okay then, we won't make it as hard. For the next fifty years, then. And only good deeds, not bad ones." (This will usually be responded to with silence.) "You're not sure if you'll live another fifty years? Well, you tell me then. How hard do you want it? I mean, you don't want to make it too easy, or you might be accused of simplistic thinking, and we can't have that! We're far too intelligent for such an accusation.

"Well, how hard do you want it?

"Isn't that ridiculous? If God accepted only people who did nothing wrong their whole life long, no one would make it into heaven. If He required even just a few selected good works from every person, there would always be someone on the earth who couldn't do one or two or more of the good deeds that God had chosen. Then God would be unfair, requiring something of some people that was impossible for them to carry out.

"In order to be fair, God had to require something that every person could do. Doesn't God have to make it as simple as possible, to give everyone an equal chance to come to Him? If faith is too simple, then the only option left is good works. That is, in fact, what other religions believe, even the most primitive. Be as good as you can and hope that it will all turn out right in the end.

"If faith is God's criterion, however, that presupposes two things. First, you have a free will. But you don't want to get to know God. You only want a god of your own making. Then it doesn't matter what God requires of you. You reject God simply on the grounds that God does not fit your own idea of what you want Him to be.

"But the real problem is pride, isn't it? Have you ever asked yourself why every religion contains a system of works as a prerequisite for entering heaven? The answer is easy. People do not want to admit that they need God. They want to be able to say to God, 'You have to let me into your heaven. I've done these good deeds, and I didn't need your help! I'm not dependent on you!'

"We are rebellious by nature and will do anything—build any kind of system—to avoid admitting our total dependence on the

God who created us. And that's the one thing God requires—
that each person give up self-pride and admit a total sinfulness
and rebellion toward God. God's condition for entering heaven
is humility and submission. God gives you a choice. He doesn't
force you to choose His method. He values you much too highly
to treat you like a robot. You can either choose simple faith in
Him and what He did for us or your own standard of good
deeds. If you choose to rely on your own good deeds, then I
have a question for you: Do you really believe that you are good
enough for God? Are you so proud and arrogant to assume that
anything you have to offer God will meet His standard of perfection and goodness?

"Would you like to read the Bible with me and discover God's
standard for letting imperfect people like you and me into heaven?"

Man Is Basically Good

"Many believe that the human race is basically good. They
point to the good deeds that have been done. Doesn't that depend on how a person determines what is 'good?' What one
person calls good might be drastically different from someone
else's definition.

"There's a difference between doing so-called 'good works'
and being 'good.' If we are basically good, why have we had so
many wars? Are those wars God's fault? Surely if history teaches
us anything about human beings it is that they are not 'good.'

"Some people believe that every person starts out with a clean
slate and then chooses to do wrong things. Then why hasn't
one single human being ever chosen *not* to do anything wrong?
Why aren't there a few, among the millions of people who have
ever lived, who have stayed perfect, as it's claimed they were at
their birth? Surely a few should have held out against wrongdo-
ing! Do you know anybody who is perfect? (These questions
will usually disarm a person.)

"Experience gives a clear picture of what human nature is
like. If we wanted to blame wars on God, then people are nothing more than an advanced microcosmic cell. People tend to

want to determine their own destiny, but they do not want to take the blame for how it turns out."

Sincerity Is Enough

"I've often heard comments like this: 'If people are sincere in their faith, I think God will let them into heaven.'

"Then shouldn't God let the Devil into heaven?" (This will usually produce a shocked expression.) "I'm sure the Devil is as sincere about his religion as any person could be."

"If you wanted to travel to a town that lay on a direct route five miles straight north of here, but you got into your car and drove straight south, you would not reach your destination. You might be the most sincere driver on the highway, committed to reaching the right town and convinced that you were heading in the right direction, but the problem is clear. You would be sincerely wrong. You would never reach the town if you didn't admit your mistake, turn around, and head in the other direction."

I Go to Church

"Why do you go to church? Why do most people go to church?" (At first, I avoid telling people which church I attend. I do not want them to put me in any religious box. That might turn them off, and then they would never read the Bible with me.)

"Some people go to church just out of habit; others go to please God. And some others go because they think that makes them Christians. That's like saying that when I walk into my garage, I become a car! Going to the airport does not mean that you can become an airplane. The airplane companies would not be happy about that, and the aviation authorities would still require you to have a license." (Note: Maintaining a light tone with laughter keeps people from getting overheated.)

"Is everyone who goes to church a good Christian? Does going to church guarantee that you will get into heaven?

"Would you like to read the Bible with me to find out what God says about going to church? Would you like to read the Bible with me to find out the proper reasons for attending church?"

The Reliability of the Bible

When I ask people if they have read the Bible, many of them will defend themselves, giving numerous reasons why they have not read it. "Studying medicine is a hard course; I am not religious; I have too much work to do; you can't understand the Bible; that's a job for a priest; I love my neighbor, and I have never done anything really bad; I'm as good as the next person."

After I have listened to their excuses, I will name some other books, completely unrelated to the Bible and not religious, and then I ask them if they have read these books. The usual reply is either "yes" or a simple "no," but they will not defend themselves.

Then I ask them why they think that they have to defend themselves for not having read the Bible. "You did not defend yourself for not reading any of those other books I named. In truth, your reasons sound far more like excuses, and it doesn't seem as though you are being honest with yourself."

The usual answer is: "You can't trust the Bible; it's outdated, unreliable; it's just like any other book." To this, respond, "If it's just like any other book, just paper and ink, why not read it like any other book? Why do you feel uncomfortable when I ask you if you have read the Bible? Why are people so afraid of a book?

"I'll tell you why people are afraid of it. Because it tells us about a man who died and rose from the dead. It also tells us what He said about life after death. But most people won't read the New Testament because they are afraid of what they might find. If, however, the Bible is true, then it seems rather stupid not to read it.

"There are two ways a person can question the authority of the Bible. If a person really wants an honest answer to his question, there are enough books on the market today that lay out the vast amount of evidence demonstrating the reliability of the Bible. I can name two books that I have found to be very comprehensive in this area. These books simply relate the facts, not theories. After a person reads these books, he has to decide what he wants to do with the facts. Many people choose to ignore them, whereas others reject them outright. Their rejection does not change the facts; it simply shows their intellectual dishonesty. Belief without a factual foundation is blindness, but a factual foundation without belief is intellectual suicide.

"If you're not asking the question out of intellectual honesty, then you're throwing that question out as an excuse for not reading the Bible. In that case, you don't really want to know if the Bible is trustworthy. When a person asks the question with this attitude, his mind is already made up. He is not willing to look at the facts because he doesn't want to know the truth. He wants to continue living in his own world of make-believe.

"Before a person can determine if a piece of literature is reliable, he has to read it for himself. To reject a book—any book— as outdated without having read it is irrational and unscientific. Have you ever read F. F. Bruce's book, *New Testament Documents: Are They Reliable?*[1] or Josh McDowell's *Evidence That Demands a Verdict?*[2] These books demonstrate that the Bible is more reliable than any other ten books combined. If you would like, we could read the Bible together and, at the same time, read one of these two books as well. The reliability of the Bible is a very important issue."

(If you have not read these two books yourself, do so as soon as possible. They are very encouraging books and will go a long way in confirming your own faith in the Word of God.)

Different Interpretations of the Bible

"People sometimes do not want to read the Bible with me because they are afraid that I will force my interpretation on them.

"I don't like telling people what is in the Bible. I know that each person can read and understand it for himself. I will tell you, though, that Jesus rejected blind faith. The things He did while He was on the earth were done to give people evidence on which to base their beliefs. Jesus tells us to be extremely skeptical of religion teachers. Anyone who claims to have a corner on the truth is suspect.

"The Bible is easier to understand than most people realize.

There are not many possible interpretations if one simply reads the Bible and lets it speak for itself. Most people don't like what the Bible has to say, so they come up with their own interpretation, one that suits their view of things.

"The Bible is the most controversial book in the world, even for those who have never read it. How can you know that it's too hard to understand when you haven't spent any time in it? Maybe all of those so-called interpretations are made up just to get away from the clear, simple, plain teaching of the Bible. How can you know if you don't read it?

"When we read it together, I won't say anything about what I think the text means. Even if you ask me a question about the meaning of something, I won't give you my answer. I'll just let you tell me what the Bible says. You can even tell me what you think it means as well, but we're more interested in what a book *says* before we can talk about what it *means*.

"When can we start reading together so that you can see how easy the Bible is to understand?"

What About the Heathen?

"I'm sure that you've asked yourself how the heathen can get to God if the Bible is the only way." (This question never fails to come up, so I raise it for them.)

"Let's assume, for the sake of argument, that God exists and that He wants to reach all people with His message. How would we go about reaching everyone in the whole world with a message?

"It would be impossible, even with our advanced methods of communication. But we are not God, and we need to be careful that we don't confine God within the limits of our capabilities. If God is God, then He would have no trouble reaching every single person in the world. Maybe He would use angels. Maybe He would send a Bible in just the right language flying through the air to land at the feet of a person who is searching for God. Maybe He would talk to each person directly. I'm not God, and I certainly don't want to demand of God that He limit His methods to ones that I can understand or approve of. Just because we don't see how something is possible doesn't mean that God is up a tree, as if He had good intentions but was helpless to carry them out.

"This question is so important that the apostle Paul answers it carefully in the book of Romans. However, Jesus lays the foundation for Romans in the Gospels. In John's gospel, Jesus gives us some very important insights into God's view of who the heathen are and how God reaches them. Romans is to the gospel of John what algebra is to basic mathematics.

"Why don't we read John, and then later Romans, to find out how the heathen can get into heaven?

If I sense that the person with whom I am talking is using this question as an escape, I usually say the following: "Wow, I didn't know you were so interested in the heathen! It's really encouraging to find someone who is concerned for more than just their own little world, someone who wants to reach out to the others who have not had the privilege of hearing about the true God. May I ask a personal question? Are you as interested in your own soul as you are in the heathen? Do you really want to know how God reaches people all over the world with His message of love and forgiveness? When can we get together to read the Bible for this answer? I think you will be very surprised at what you'll find there."

Why Does God Allow Evil?

Some people reject God because they claim that He is to blame for the evil in the world. (Basically, this is the opposite of the previous argument.)

"If God is a loving God, some people say, then He would not allow all of the evil in the world. Has God caused all of the wars that are going on? Are we just robots that are being manipulated by a vicious God? Do you think that *you* are a robot? Who is more likely to have caused these wars, people or God?

"The Bible gives us in Romans a very good answer to the question about evil. Before we tackle Romans, however, why don't we read John together and see what Jesus says about suffering there? Jesus gives some enlightening answers to this question, especially in chapters 9 and 11. Because we do not want to take anything out of context, let's start reading at chapter 1. That way we won't miss anything. When can we start reading together?"

(If you would like further and more exhaustive answers to this subject, read C. S. Lewis's book *The Problem of Pain*[3] and Philip Yancey's *Where Is God When It Hurts?*[4] Read these books, but do not let the understandings you gain from them get in the way of your reading the Bible with your unsaved friend.)

Is One Religion as Good as Another?

"Of what religion are you? Why do you belong to that religion?" (The person might say, "I was born into it," or "my parents belong to it," or "I joined it out of conviction." In any case, the goal of your question is the same: Find out how the person differentiates his or her personal faith from all other religions.)

"What makes your religion different from other religions? Why do you think that your religion is the right one—just because you were born into it? Many religious people believe this: Muslims, Buddhists, Catholics, and Protestants. Millions of people believe what they have been taught. Does that guarantee that they'll get to heaven? Does that make your religion the right one?

"Do you believe what the theologians teach? Why? How do you know if the theologians are right? How do the theologians determine what is right or wrong? Do you let others tell you what to believe?

"One religion might be as good as any other religion, but if they are all the same, then it doesn't make any difference what a person believes. And if they are all right, then we have absolutely no way of knowing if there is life after death, if there is a heaven or a hell, or even if there is a God! I'm not criticizing any religion. I'm just asking how you know that your religion is the right one.

"Don't all religions have a system of theology? If each religion has its own theology, how can I know which theology is right? Even among the so-called Christians, there are vast differences of opinion. They can't all be right, can they? Which theologians should I trust? I believe that a person should read the Bible personally. I'm a skeptic at heart, and I don't believe what others have to say about the Bible. I have learned to ask myself, 'How do I know that they are telling me the truth and not just their version of the truth?'

"The issues at stake are not trivial. For instance, is there life after death? What is God really like? If we were to combine all of the religions in the world, do we expect God to be a combination of all of them? Is there a heaven or a hell, and if so, what does God require of me so that I can go to heaven? Can I know now, before I die, where I'm going after death? These are eternal questions, and they warrant serious consideration." (Your friend might give reasons for not reading the Bible. If so, emphasize the preceding paragraph.)

"Is any belief good enough to get me into heaven? What if I believe that the sun is going to shine tomorrow and it really happens—will this belief get me into heaven? Is simply believing that God exists enough to get a person into heaven?

"When people compare religions, they usually compare followers of those religions, Christians with Muslims, for example. I don't think that's logical. Nobody in any religion claims to be perfect. If they do, we have sanatoriums for them. If we want to find out if a specific religion is from God, we need to go to the founder of that religion and compare his teaching with his lifestyle. Does he preach a good line, requiring everyone to follow what he says? Does he live according to his own teachings? None of us wants to follow a hypocrite. If we are searching for God, then we want to be sure that we have found Him before we commit ourselves to following someone who claims to represent God.

"We also need to compare his teachings and lifestyle with those of the founders of other religions. If you have ever read the New Testament and the Koran, you would immediately run across some very interesting comparisons between Muhammad and Jesus." (I usually stop here and let that last comment sink in. If my friend is really searching for God, that statement will stir curiosity to ask more questions, and we will end up reading the gospel of John together. If not, the person will come up with more arguments for not reading the Bible.)

"Would you like to read the Bible with me to find out what kind of person Jesus Christ was? Would you like to read the Bible with me to learn about true Christianity as opposed to false professing Christianity?"

Everyone Wants to Go to Heaven

"What is heaven like? Most people have no idea what heaven will be like. Some people might even be surprised to discover that they won't like what heaven is like.

"Most people assume that heaven is some nebulous place where everything is perfect. They seem to realize that only God is perfect, which means that heaven is perfect because God is there. Instead of asking ourselves what heaven is like, shouldn't we really be asking what *God* is like? Is that what you expect from heaven—to be with God forever?" (The importance of this concept should not be overlooked. I will pause to let this idea, which will be new to most people, sink in.)

"If being in heaven is the same as being with God, can I know a little bit about what God is like now, before I die? We wouldn't want to be too surprised. Maybe our ideas of God are all wrong, and maybe we won't like Him as He really is. Or worse yet, what if God doesn't like us as we are!

"It seems to me that most people want to go to heaven—as long as God is not there! They want God's gifts, but they do not want God. They take the physical life that God has given them freely; they enjoy the sun and the rain; they breathe the air—giving no thought to its source—but they have no time for God. Why should God let such people into His heaven?

"Would you like to read the Bible with me to discover what heaven is like? Would you like to read the Bible with me to discover what God is like, so you won't be surprised when you meet Him?"

Hope

The subject of hope can be an easy door into conversations about spiritual things. I have listed some of the topics I have used as a springboard for talking about the futility of false hope.

Politics. "When we have the next election, I hope the winning candidate is sinless."

Weather. [In July] "I hope it snows today." (This only applies to those living in the appropriate latitudes.)

Science. "I hope the scientists will stop building atomic weapons."

Homemaking. "When I get home today, I hope the house has been repainted, the carpets cleaned, the dishes washed, the kids have done their homework without being yelled at ten times," and so on.

Academic Studies or School. "I haven't studied in weeks, but I hope I get an 'A' on the final exam." (This one might not be the best one to use; a few brainy people are running around who don't study and still pass all the tests.)

Health. "I hope to stay healthy for two hundred years. I hope that I can grow some hair on my head" (bald person speaking).

History. "I hope that there won't be another war" (amidst the dozen or so about which we hear every day in the news).

I will illustrate the use of this last topic, history. The world had twenty years of peace between World War I and World War II. Since World War II, we have had more than forty years of "world peace," although the number of wars in individual countries has increased dramatically. No one wants to have another world war, which may very well be nuclear in nature, and during a time of peace most people do not care to think seriously about the consequences of a nuclear war. When I am in a conversation with someone and the subject of war comes up, I usually ask if he thinks that humankind can avoid World War III. The usual answer is, "I hope so."

This brings us around to the subject of hope. I continue the conversation by giving the following illustration, which can be used no matter with what topic you started. "Suppose that we are sitting in a restaurant in Washington, D.C. What would you think if I told you that I 'hoped' to be in London within the next five minutes? You would probably politely turn me off and not want to speak with me again. If you were a close friend, you might ask me how long I have had this problem. And you would be right, if I really meant it. But what is wrong with my hope of being in London in the next five minutes? That's simple. It's not physically possible. In other words, I have no basis for my hope. My hope is grounded on thin air, on my imagination and nothing more. One could say that my hope was 'hopeless.'

"It's the same with hoping that there won't be another war in Europe for another forty years. History shows that there is a high probability another war will occur in Europe in the not-so-distant future. Some people will answer that they don't believe that there will be another war because people have become intelligent enough to know that war is futile.

"They might be right, but in the 1930s and 1940s some of the most intelligent human beings that the world has ever produced were Nazis. They used their intelligence to massacre millions of people. In their case, they used their intelligence negatively. The world would have been better off if these people had been less intelligent!

"The most commonly used word in Europe in 1939 was the word 'peace.' Today, we have only to look at Central America, Afghanistan, or the Middle East to see 'intelligent' humanity at peace with itself. And what will happen when a political fanatic finally acquires the atomic bomb? How can we still hope that there won't be another war?

"For hope to be realistic, it has to be grounded on something solid. Human nature and human intelligence are two of the worst foundations we could pick."

The Future

Planning for the future provides a good introduction for talking about spiritual things. As with the subject of hope, any number of topics can be used to introduce the subject of the future, including the following.

Studies. "I'm planning to finish my studies by next year."

Employment. "I'm planning to change jobs next month." Or, "I'm planning to retire by the time I'm sixty."

Family. "We're planning to start our family after we are financially more stable."

The list could go on indefinitely. The questions I have listed can be used at any time. The conversation might go like this:

"How far into the future do you plan? Everyone plans for the future. Why are you studying? Why do people study at all? Do you just want to get a good job? Do you want more from life than what your parents had? Do you want to become famous or make some great scientific discovery for the progress of humanity? All of these goals concern the future. The plans you make for the future determine how you live now.

"Some people tell me that they just live for 'now.' If they are honest with themselves, they usually see that any definition of 'now' is a period of time. That period might be shorter for some and longer for others, but everyone lives for the future. Even the alcoholic on the street asks himself regularly where he is going to get the next bottle. His future is only a day or less.

"Why do you study for tests? You want to pass them and go

on to the next ones and eventually graduate. Why? You'll want to get a good job, eventually get married, and support a family. Can you imagine what your wife would say if you said, 'I just live for now, so I'm not going to work today'? How long would your marriage last if you never planned for the future?

"When will you start planning for retirement? Some people say that you can't start planning for retirement too soon. Put in capsule form, life seems rather short, doesn't it?

"The important question to ask is how far into the future you will plan. You can buy house insurance, fire insurance, health insurance, and life insurance, but you can't buy *eternal* life insurance. Most people live only for the future in *this* life, but what about after death? We live for seventy years but are dead forever. Why don't we plan for that future? Why are our sights so short?

"The answer is simple. Most people have no idea what life after death is like, so they just don't think about it. But shouldn't we at least ask if anyone is qualified to tell us if there is life after death, and what kind of life it is?

"If you answer, 'I suppose you're going to say that God is qualified,' do you know a better person to whom to go for the answer? If you're a skeptic or antireligious, then we could compare what the different religions say about life after death. Very few religions, however, have a concrete idea of what life after death is like. The Bible gives us a clear picture of eternal life, and if you're interested, I would be glad to read the New Testament with you to discover the answer."

Freedom and Morals

A student once said to me, "I want to live as I want, without God laying all of His moral laws and legalistic commands on me. I want to remain absolutely free." My argument went as follows.

"First, there's no such thing as absolute freedom. We have discovered that we are limited within our physical world by laws of physics. Take gravity, for instance. Without it, we would all fly off the earth. Our solar system couldn't stay together. At the same time, if we try to reject this law, there will be immediate consequences. Try stepping out of your window" (we were high up in an apartment building) "and see if you have absolute freedom from our physical laws.

"Every country in the world has laws that have to be kept if people are to live in peace with those around them. The examples could go on and on. Fish have freedom to exist—as long as they stay in the water. Can you imagine a fish saying, 'I think I'll go for a walk on land today'? That fish has to remain within the bounds of his limitations—his natural laws—or the consequence is death. A train has the freedom to go anywhere it wants—as long as it stays on the tracks. Sports teams can't go out onto the field and play the game any way they choose. They have to follow the rules, or they will be disqualified. The game would make no sense whatsoever if neither team played by the rules.

"Staying healthy requires that we have a balanced lifestyle, eat properly, sleep enough, and get adequate exercise. No one is free from pain or suffering. If we did not feel pain when we cut ourselves, we could bleed to death without knowing it. We need pain. It tells us when something is wrong and needs to be corrected.

"Why is it, then, if we are limited in all of these areas of our lives, that we demand absolute freedom in our *moral* lives? A scientist would look at all of these areas and conclude that the probability of our having absolute freedom is minimal.

"In the first place, we need laws and limitations to survive. If we did not have them, we would cease to exist. On the other hand, if we break these laws, we pay the price of negative consequences.

"What if this is also true in the area of moral laws? What if God made His moral laws for our good, just as He made the physical law of gravity for our good? What if God gave us moral laws because He loves us and doesn't want us to reap the negative consequences of an immoral life? What if the consequences of breaking His moral laws are equally as devastating as breaking

His laws of gravity—death? If a person cannot have peace with those in his society when he breaks society's laws, can that person have peace with God when he breaks God's moral laws?

"Maybe you believe that each person should be able to determine which morals are right for him, and no one else should be able to tell him that his morals are wrong. If this were true, I could take your girlfriend and make her live with me, and you could not tell me I was wrong. Those would be the morals I had chosen for me. And if you tried to stop me, then whichever one of us was stronger would win, just as it is in the animal kingdom. No one is right or wrong, just strong or weak, mean or nice.

"You might accuse me of being a legalistic puritan, but don't I have the 'freedom' to live a moral life for the sake of those I love? Won't my wife appreciate my faithfulness? Won't my children be happier if I choose to love only my wife and never get divorced? Won't my children have a healthier view of marriage if I treat my wife like a queen her whole life? Don't I have the right to give my wife and my children a happy and secure family life? If you ever get married, will you still have the same moral freedoms as you demand now? If you say no, how will your wife trust you when you haven't had high morals before marriage? And if you do not have high morals, how can you object if one day you discover that your wife has a couple of lovers on the side?

"Is that your idea of absolute freedom?"

Death and Suicide

As a school bus driver in college, I had contact with many young people. I spoke to one young man about God, but he said that he was not interested in the spiritual side of life yet. One day, he asked me if I could help his younger brother get off drugs. A few days earlier, the brother had talked about committing suicide. He said that he had talked to him but that his younger brother would not listen. Could I talk some sense into him? The conversation went as follows.

"Why should I help your younger brother get off drugs? Maybe your brother has tried a number of things seeking happiness, and the best thing he has found so far has been drugs. Why do you want to take his happiness away from him? The only reason you should get him off drugs is to give him something better, something that will make him happier than drugs do. What do you have to offer him?

"You've rejected my offer to learn more about God, but you want me to talk to your brother. Why do you want your brother to learn about God, but you, his older example, reject this idea for yourself? If he wants to commit suicide, and because you have nothing better to offer him, he will assume that your life has no more meaning than his, and he won't listen to you when you tell him that suicide is wrong. Maybe he really would be happier dead; how can you know he won't?

"I would be glad to talk to your brother. Maybe I can point him toward Jesus and help him find what he's searching for: real meaning in life. You obviously can't give it to him. If you really want to help your brother, you need to give your life to the Lord. Then you'll have something to offer, and he might begin to listen to you."

For further conversation starters on the subject of death, refer to chapter 5.

DO IT!

1. Most of your conversations will not follow those you have read about in this chapter, but I have written them as thought stimulants to show you how to direct different conversations with your unsaved friends. Do not try to use these talks verbatim. Modify them to fit your own personality and your own friends.

2. Plan to have one conversation this week with an unsaved friend and use at least one of the conversations in this chapter. Modify it to fit! Think through your friend's possible answers and how you can respond with further questions or comments that will make this person think further. Phone your friend.

3. How would you respond to the following comment from an unsaved friend? "I'll wait until I'm older to think about God and eternal life." Write several questions and try them out.

Chapter 12

"He Said Yes!"

Reading the Bible with a Friend

You've finally done it! You've talked a friend into reading the Bible with you. Praise the Lord! Now comes the question: How should you read together? Should you explain every word in every verse? Should you show your friend all of the cross-references from Genesis to Revelation on each verse? What if he asks a question and you don't know the answer?

The first thing is to relax. You want your friend to enjoy reading with you, instead of feeling as though you're pushing something onto him. If you decide to meet in your home, do whatever you must to make him feel comfortable and at home. Serve snacks (such as chips or peanuts) and some coffee, tea, or soft drinks. Sometimes people are afraid that they will be captured and sucked into a cult if they attend a Bible study in someone else's home. If you sense this in your friend, offer to come to his house. Sacrifice some of your time, drive over to his home, and hold the Bible study there. Ask him to determine the time (if your work schedule will allow it) and place, so that he will not feel threatened or frightened. Remember, Jesus ate and drank with sinners, and He was glad to do it. We can visit our unsaved friends without becoming contaminated.

Actually, the key to reading the Bible with a friend is simple: Ask questions on every verse, questions that anyone can easily answer simply by reading the text. Do not go into lengthy theological discussions about Greek verb tenses. Your friend needs to be shown that anyone can understand the basics of the Bible message without years of theological education.

In chapter 15 I have written out numerous questions and ideas on the first few verses of John's gospel to get you started. I have not written a complete commentary on the gospel of John. This section is for those who want to lead their friends into a simple Bible study, without using anything but the Bible itself. I have tried to demonstrate how to ask good questions during a Bible study, questions that will force the participants to think for themselves. Do your best to *study the passage beforehand,* reading it a number of times, making some notes, and then leaving this book at home. You want to instill in your friends the belief that they can understand the Bible without a theologian or Bible teacher telling them what to believe.

You probably won't use all of the questions or comments that I have written. This study is not meant to be used word for word. It will have served its purpose if you can use it to help your friends think about the Bible text for themselves. As you learn how to ask questions, you will think of your own questions to fit your own friends.

My unsaved friends have raised the following questions and objections during our studies, and I have provided the answers that I gave in an effort to continue discussing the text at hand without getting sidetracked.

What do you do when someone asks a question and expects you to answer it immediately? You simply say, "That's a good question, and the answer is in the Bible" (maybe Romans or Ephesians). "However, I don't want to answer that question right now because the answer is not found in our present text. I prefer that you find the answers in the proper context. I don't want to take one or two verses out of a different context in the Bible to answer your question."

"Yes, but you've read the Bible and know the answers, so I'm asking you."

"Thank you for that vote of confidence, but I have a question for you. Why should you believe my answer? Maybe I belong to some weird cult. Maybe I really want to win your confidence and then rob you of your money."

If someone persists, simply say, "If you want a prefabricated belief, in which you don't need to think for yourself, then go to any local church or cult and tell them that you want to be told what to believe. I'm not going to do that to you. I want you to come to your own conclusions about what you are reading. I never want to hear you say, 'I reject what Floyd [Insert your own name here, please, not mine!] says about the Bible.' Please believe me. What *I* have to say about the Bible is worthless to you. I might not understand something in the Bible correctly, and it would be a sad mistake for you to rely on *me* for your chance at eternity. The important thing is that you find out what God really meant when He wrote His book."

Don't get sidetracked by having to answer questions that are not answered in the current text. Many people cannot understand the answers anyway until they have read and understood more of the simple things in the Gospels. If you can anticipate their questions, tell them their questions before they ask them. For instance, you might say at the outset, "If the Bible is true, and Jesus is the only way to heaven, what about the heathen in Africa? How does God propose to save them? This question is answered very clearly in Romans chapter 1, which we will get to after we have finished John."

Letting them see that you already know the questions they have will show them that you are a critical thinker and that you are ahead of them. Don't, however, give them the answers to their questions. Just tell them where to find the answers in the Bible (if you know; if you don't, say so) and keep reading John. Tell them that they can read any other books in the Bible if they want.

One man asked me the question about the heathen, and I

gave him the aforementioned answer. He got angry and said, "Well, I'll just read Romans myself this week!" I told him to go ahead. He came back the next week and said, "I read Romans. I didn't understand it. Let's keep going in John."

The following questions and answers should help you avoid subjects that are too advanced for your friend at first.

> *Question:* "Is the Bible reliable? How can you trust the Bible when it's so outdated?"
> *Answer:* "That is a very important question, and we will have to answer it at some point in our study. However, how can a person know if any book is trustworthy if he hasn't first read the book for himself? Let's finish reading John and then ask that question again later."

> *Question:* "Is Christ the only way to God?"
> *Answer:* "John 14 gives us a direct answer to that question. But let's finish the first thirteen chapters first so we aren't pulling John 14 out of its context."

> *Question:* "How are miracles possible?"
> *Answer:* "That's a good question but not the right one. The right questions are: 'Does God exist as a supernatural being? If so, is it possible for us as finite human beings to understand how God does His miracles?' We certainly don't believe that something is impossible just because we don't understand it, do we? That would be incredibly arrogant on our part."

Remember that when they disagree with what the Bible says, you should not defend it or your view that the Bible is right. The Bible *is* right regardless of whether they believe it. The Holy Spirit will convict them, and He will defend it much better, through their conscience, than we can. Simply tell them, "I didn't write the Bible, and it might not be to your liking, but that's what it says. Whether you choose to accept or reject it is your decision. Our question should not be, 'Do I agree with it?' but rather, 'Is it right?' It makes no difference if you reject me or my views. Everything—your whole eternity—hangs on whether you accept or reject Jesus and what He says."

Question: "What about the heathen?"
Answer: Previous answers might suffice, but if your friend is belligerent, you might say jokingly, "Wow! I didn't know you were so missionary-minded! I didn't know you had such a strong concern for the souls of the heathen. Are you equally concerned about your own soul? I want to know first where *I'm* going when I die, and then I'll worry about the heathen. Maybe you and I are heathens and don't know it!"

Question: "How can a loving God let the innocent suffer, especially children?"
Answer: "That's a very good question, but we need to be sure that we really want God, and not some theologian, to answer it. I'm sure that we could have an interesting discussion about defining the concept of *innocence,* but the most complete answer God gives to that question is found in the book of Job in the Old Testament. Job asked the very same question, and God gave him some incredible answers. We'll even find one of those answers when we get to John 9. Are you sure that you want God's answer to that question? What if you don't like His answer?"

Question: "Do I need to be baptized?"
Answer: "John the Baptist and Jesus both have something to say about baptism."

If someone persists in wanting answers, ask, "Can a ten-year-old child understand university-level physics? Of course not. He hasn't studied all of the prerequisites. If you had to read a physics book for your own employment, would you understand the whole book after one reading? I wouldn't!"

Some people might laugh at this, and you should laugh with them, then continue.

"Please don't think that the whole Bible is easy to understand with just one reading. God didn't make it that easy. I don't claim to have all of the answers, but the ones I do have, I didn't get overnight.

"Your questions are very good. Most people seem to have given up thinking. Your questions show that you haven't. Excellent! Some of your questions, however, can be answered only after you have grasped the basics of what Jesus is saying in the Gospels. The letters of Paul and Peter and John are all based on knowledge of the Gospels. It's very difficult to understand some of the answers to our questions when we jump all over the Bible, instead of reading through it systematically, just as we would read a novel."

I told a philosophy professor once that he could not understand the answer to one of his questions until he had personally met the person who had the answer.

He replied, "You mean, Jesus?"

When I said yes, he folded his arms and said, "Well, I'm not going to read any further with you until I get the answer."

We were eating lunch together in a crowded restaurant, and I laughed out loud at his response. I said, "I don't believe this! If you asked me a question, and I told you that the only person in the world who had the answer lived in China, and that you would have to go and meet him personally to get the answer, would you fold your arms like a little child (I folded my arms as he had done) and tell me that you had to have the answer to the question before you were willing to go meet the only man who had the answer? What kind of philosophical logic is that?"

A number of people had turned to listen to our conversation, and he turned a little red. After a pause, he said, "Read on."

Tell your friends, "The Bible will answer all of your questions but not in the first few chapters of John. John does answer some of the important questions in the universe, however. We won't find a lack of answers if we just tune in to God's questions. Keep reading. I'm still finding answers to my own questions."

"But you have read the Bible so much!" they might say. "How can you have more questions?"

"I have a wall in my mind. This wall has hundreds of nails stuck into it. Every time I have a question with no answer, I mentally hang the question on one of those nails, and I keep reading and studying.

"Every now and then, I go to the wall and look over the questions. And every time, I discover that some of those questions, through the course of time and study, have been answered. Having questions with no answers does not cause me to give up reading and studying; it motivates me to go on. No student of physics or psychology or any other subject would quit his studies simply because he does not have all of the answers to his questions all at once."

If your friend has a question and you do not know the answer, say so! Tell him, "That's a question that is still hanging on the wall. I don't have the answer—yet—but I will some day. Let's keep reading."

One final point. Don't push too hard for a decision. Let the Holy Spirit do that. Continually ask the following questions.

- Do they really understand what sin is?
- Do they really want to follow the Lord?
- Do they really want the Lord—or just His gifts?
- Are they really far enough?

Don't accept their first announcement that they believe. Their first decision might not be a decision to accept the Lord as their Savior but merely a decision to read on, to start thinking more.

May the Lord bless your time together!

DO IT!

1. Pray that your friend will read the Bible with you for at least three months.
2. Read John's gospel every day for your own preparation.
3. Celebrate privately and thank the Lord that your friend said yes.

Chapter 13

What If My Friend Says No?

"No, I'm not really interested in reading the Bible with you."

How do we respond when our friend says this in response to our invitation to read the Bible with us?

First, we have to keep the scriptural perspective in mind. Not everyone will want to read the Bible with us. Jesus said in John 7:17, "If any man is willing to do His will, he shall know of the teaching, whether it is of God, or whether I speak from Myself." A person has to *want* to find God before a proper response is possible. Matthew 7:13-14 is frightening but true: "Enter by the narrow gate; for the gate is wide, and the way is broad that leads to destruction, and many are those who enter by it. For the gate is small, and the way is narrow that leads to life, and few are those who find it." We cannot expect everyone to say yes, when, in fact, most people will probably say no.

When the rich young ruler came to Jesus and asked what he had to do to receive eternal life, he rejected the Lord's answer. When he walked away, Jesus didn't chase after him and say, "No, wait. Come back. Let me make it easier for you." Nor did He force a decision on him. The gospel is not ours to water down; it is for us to proclaim.

There is at least one good alternative that we can offer to an unsaved friend, however. If your friend says no to reading the Bible with you, ask him to read it on his own. If he says yes to this suggestion, then ask if you could get together with him later

165

to hear what he thinks about what he has read. I learn much from my unsaved friends' viewpoints. I tell them that I am interested in their view of the Bible because it helps me to understand them, and sometimes I am motivated to revise my own view of a certain passage because others have shared their thoughts with me. I am still learning, and I have a lot to learn from them.

If your friend chooses neither to read the Bible with you nor even to give the Bible much thought, that does not mean that your friend will not respond to the gospel later. We all want to be surprised when we arrive in heaven to find that our unsaved friends and relatives did, even in the final moments of their lives, accept the Lord. We will most certainly discover that our prayers played a vital role in finally motivating others to let go of their pride and to give their lives to the Lord Jesus. Never assume that an unsaved person is going to stay unsaved just because he or she is not willing to respond to the gospel when you present it.

The key to motivating your friend in the future can depend on your Christian lifestyle. Have you really changed, or is this new religious discovery just a short-lived hobbyhorse.

Before Helmut got saved, he had alienated all of his relatives and most of his friends with his temper and crudeness. Within a few days after accepting the Lord, he had further alienated his six relatives by "evangelizing" them. He finally came to the conclusion that his family was unreachable by this method, and he asked me what he should do. I told him to stop talking to them about his new-found faith and to begin to listen to their views. Also, he should start being nice to them by doing things for them that they would appreciate. He began by giving his wife some flowers. She nearly died of a heart attack! He spent a weekend working on his brother's house while his brother was out of town on business. When his brother returned, he didn't believe that it was Helmut who had done the work.

A year later, his sister called me and said, "Mr. Schneider, my brother has changed too much for this to be another one of his weird ideas. There has to be something about the Bible that can change a person so much. Is there a Bible study for me to attend somewhere in my area?"

It took one year for the first breakthrough. At the time of this writing, three of his relatives are believers. Helmut had learned to love his relatives instead of preaching to them.

I heard a story a few years ago about a man, Robert, who accepted the Lord when in his early forties and was immediately rejected by his two other brothers and disinherited by his elderly and very wealthy grandfather. Robert continued to show love to his brothers and visited his grandfather often. He eventually got his grandfather to read the Bible. Shortly before he died, the grandfather accepted the Lord.

At the reading of the grandfather's will, the two brothers discovered, to their delight, that the grandfather had left everything to them and nothing to Robert. To their amazement, Robert said that he did not want to contest the will. He said that he had his grandfather—he would see him in heaven—and that was enough for him.

A week later, two things happened on the same day. One of the brothers called Robert to ask why he had chosen not to contest the will. They set a time to get together to discuss it. Robert also told him that it had to do with Jesus and the Bible and that he would bring a Bible for his brother to start reading. The brother agreed. A little while later, Robert received a letter from the lawyer. The grandfather had given the lawyer the following instructions: "Robert is to receive nothing. I know him well enough to know that Jesus and I are more important to him than my money. I am positive that he will not contest the will. I also know my other two greedy grandsons. I am convinced that the only way Robert can reach them is by *showing* them that there is more to life than their money.

"If Robert does refuse to contest the will, then he is to receive the enclosed modest [six figures!] savings account for his business. If I have misjudged Robert and he does contest the will, the savings account is to be given to a charity."

I do not know if Robert's brothers have become Christians, but I am sure that Robert and his grandfather are going to have a splendid reunion.

Continue loving the friend who still refuses to read with you. Always be available when needed, even if just to talk over the fence about the weather.

My wife spent months cultivating the friendship of our next-door neighbor (a homemaker and university instructor). The woman accepted my wife's friendship warmly and gladly but constantly rejected any conversations about our faith. She went so far as to protect her husband from any private conversation with me. But on the opposite track, she sent her two daughters to our church's Sunday school—so that she could sleep longer on Sunday mornings. Seeing her lifestyle and pride, we predicted how things would turn out for her, and we were right: Her husband filed for divorce a couple of years after we moved to another town. She was still closed to the gospel, but a mutual friend has been in contact with her husband and reports that he has become interested in spiritual things.

Sometimes the Lord will use a tragedy or a failure to bring an unsaved person to seek Him. Sometimes people respond correctly, and sometimes they become more bitter. Sometimes we are surprised by the interest of someone other than the person for whom we've been praying. Our only hope is continued prayer.

So do you stop being a friend when people say no? Definitely not! My wife and I have never stopped being friends with someone who would not read the Bible with us. Although we have continued to invite them over or offered to help them in some way, very few of our unsaved friends who said no have wanted to continue spending time with us after they discovered that we were "religious." *They* stopped spending time with *us; we never* closed the door on them. Keep your door open and keep praying for them.

DO IT!

1. If you have been doing all of the "Do It!" sections at the end of each chapter, you are probably already reading the Bible with an unsaved friend. If, however, a friend has said no, and you have not picked someone else to ask, go back to your friend and give her a New Testament to read on her own. Then make her the offer found in this chapter.
2. Keep praying for this friend.
3. Ask others to pray for this friend.
4. Ask another unsaved friend to read with you.

Chapter 14

The Diving Board

Time to Jump In!

As I said at the beginning, this book is not the final word on evangelism. There are other methods of evangelism. The best method is the method that *works,* and a believer should be ready and willing to use any appropriate, honest method of evangelism that will bring people to the Lord. In any case, our unsaved friends have to be brought under the Word of God and faced with the decision to give their lives to Christ. I prefer to have them read the Bible with me. If you prefer a different approach, use it to God's glory.

I have experienced three stages at which people give up reading the Bible with me. Most of them stop after the first time. Once seems to be enough for them. Others make it as far as John 4, and then they give up. They stumble over the biblical teaching that "belief" is equated with "obedience" in John 3:36. A few readers continue on through John 6, and then they, too, finally call it quits. Maybe we can see a pattern here because many of the Lord's disciples left him in John 6:66.

It usually takes from six to nine months to read as far as John 6. If you have finished these six chapters in ten weeks, your friend might not really understand the gospel and its main ramification (obedience!). So do not be in hurry to finish John's gospel. Give the Holy Spirit time to convict your friend. Repentance is the goal, not superficial verbal assent to the gospel.

Once you have reached the end of chapter 6 with your friend, he or she will probably decide whether to continue. If your friend chooses to continue, be encouraged. Almost everyone who has started reading the Bible with me and continued into chapter 7 has become a believer. Don't give up! Even after he or she becomes a believer, finish John's gospel before jumping into something deeper. Your friend needs a strong, basic foundation before deeper theology (milk before meat).

May the Lord richly bless your endeavors to lead your friends into the kingdom of our Lord Jesus Christ.

DO IT!

1. Have you done it?

Chapter 15

Commentary/Questions/ Ideas on John 1–6

Remember to ask questions, give people time to think about each question, and do not give them answers. Let the text speak for itself. Don't worry if you don't know the answers to all of the questions I have mentioned; just use them to get others thinking and talking. It doesn't matter, at first, what everyone says as long as each person is taking part. Use your own open Bible and be sure that each person has one, too. Don't use this book. You want people to get used to having a Bible in their hands and learning their way around in it as you have done.

John 1:1-18

The entire gospel is contained in these first eighteen verses. You should spend a lot of time reading and rereading them alone before asking an unsaved friend to join you.

John 1:1-5

[1]In the beginning was the Word, and the Word was with God, and the Word was God.

[2]He was in the beginning with God.

[3]All things came into being through Him; and apart from Him nothing came into being that has come into being.

⁴In Him was life; and the life was the light of men.

⁵And the light shines in the darkness; and the darkness did not comprehend [overpower] it.

Verse 1: How does John prove the existence of God? He doesn't! He assumes that the reader believes in God's existence. People cannot prove that God exists, nor can they prove that God does not exist. Either view requires faith.

A translation student told me that he didn't believe in God because he hadn't met Him. I asked him if he had had all the experiences of every person who had lived. He said no. Then I asked if it were possible that God lay outside of his experience. When he said yes, I told him that God lay inside my experience, and that he should beware of assuming that something does not exist just because he didn't know anything about it.

A small boy once turned on the light switch in his room and asked his mother, "Mommy, where does that light come from?"

She replied, "A man put wires in our house when it was built, and the electricity comes through the wires."

He responded, "I don't believe that a man put wires in our house. I believe the light and the switch were always there." Many adults act like that little boy when they accept the fact that they can install electricity into a house but reject the fact that God made electricity.

Why does John call God the Word? What is a word? To what purpose do we use words? We use words to communicate something to someone else. What does God want to communicate? The text does not say, "God *had* the Word," but "God *was* the Word." What is the difference between the two statements?

If I came to you and said, "I have a word for you," what would you think I meant? You would probably think that I had a message to give you. But what if I came to you and said, "I *am* the word for you." You might think about calling the men in white jackets and having me hauled off for psychiatric help.

The difference is clear. If I say, "I *am* the word for you," I mean that I want you to know me personally. Does God want us to know Him personally? Does God want to communicate *Himself* to you and to me?

God doesn't just want to tell us facts, like a boring teacher in the classroom. He calls Himself the Word. He wants to communicate Himself. Do we believe that?

Is God really personal? If He is, isn't it logical that God can communicate with us as we do with one another? How does a person speak with an impersonal force? Read the second conversation in chapter 6 again. The illustration about finding God in nature can be used effectively in John 1.

An unsaved person might say that, even if God is personal, He doesn't talk to us in the same way we talk to each other. Why, then, do we write letters if not to "talk" to one another?

Does God want to tell *me* about Himself?

I asked a professor this question once, and he replied, "I can't believe that God wants to reveal Himself to me personally. I'm a nothing, and He has far more important things to think about."

I asked him if he wanted a God who concerned Himself with each individual.

He responded, "Very much so, but that's just a dream."

"Not if the Bible is true," I added, and went on to the next question. This question and the answer will show our friends how easy the Bible is to understand.

Some people will get philosophical and look for deep and difficult answers. Encourage them to think simply. I did not try to prove that the Bible is true. I just left him with that statement in his mind.

If God wants to communicate something to us, doesn't it have to be very simple for us to understand? Can we imagine God sitting in heaven, looking down on us in disgust because of our incredible ignorance? Out of His mercy, however, He stoops and chooses two or three of the most intelligent of these advanced "apes." He says to the first one, "Well, since you have a theological education, I'll choose you." To the second, He says, "You took so many tests while you were studying at the university, I might as well choose you, too." To the third He says, "You're not too bright, but you're probably smarter than all of those other donkeys down there. I guess I'll just have to make do and tell you three what I want the rest of humanity to know." Doesn't that sound ridiculous?

Many theologians will tell you that you need years of Greek and Hebrew and a lot of theology before you can even begin to understand the Bible. But if God wants to speak to each of us, He, being far more intelligent than we are, would have to communicate with us very simply. If God has spoken to us through the Bible, then even the most simple of people should be able to understand it.

My family went to Greece for two weeks one summer, and there we met a man from Holland who taught Greek to ten- and eleven-year-olds. I asked him if they ever read New Testament Greek. He laughed and said, "The children read New Testament Greek as bedtime stories. That's about the easiest Greek there is."

My wife commented to me afterward, "Isn't it interesting that God wrote His book so simply that even children can understand it?"

How could the Word be with God and be God at the same time? The answer is quite simple. Jesus as a person was with God the Father in all of eternity past. Jesus is also God the Son, as He is called later in this gospel. Don't give the people at the Bible study this answer! Tell them that the answer is in John's gospel, and they will have to find it for themselves. Tell them over and over that they must not come to depend upon you, the Bible study leader, as their answer person. At the very first meeting, start instilling in them the need to find the answers for themselves from the text. This requirement will play a vital role in their own maturing process once they have become believers.

Verse 2: What beginning is John talking about? Our friends might say, "The beginning of time," to which you could reply, "What existed before time?" They might say, "It was before anything existed," to which you might ask, "Did God have a beginning?" It doesn't matter what their answer is so long as you get them thinking about the verse. Do not give them your answers or opinions. After you have talked about this verse and their answers for a while, go on to the next verse.

Verse 3: What does the word *all* in verse 3 mean? We didn't come together to discuss evolution versus the Bible, but we need to see from the very beginning that the Bible might not agree with everything that the scientists want us to believe. The sciences, after all, are "observational," that is, we build our laws of physics or biology on what we observe. More often than not, the scientists have to revamp and rethink these fallible scientific laws because they turn out to be incorrect as a result of newly discovered information. Every scientist realizes that the human race has not observed everything there is to observe. There are big holes in our understanding of our universe. Any scientist who is honest will tell us that the more we learn about our universe, the more we realize how little we know.

If God did write the Bible (through men), then He should know more than we do about this universe that He planned and created. I'm not saying that the Bible is a science textbook, but when it makes statements about "our" sciences, we should be careful not to assume automatically that these statements are false because they seem to contradict our very limited knowledge of this universe. If there is a God who made the universe, He has had many a laugh at our arrogant announcements that we have finally discovered the secret of a certain aspect of science only to have to revise our "established facts" later and admit that they were only theories all along. Even if we assume that evolution is correct, there remain two questions unanswered by this theory. Where did the material world come from in the first place, and how did dead matter turn itself into living matter? Neither of these questions can be answered by evolution. The answers can only be assumed if we rely solely on our observational sciences. If, however, we take into account all of the evidence (information that comes from outside our own experience, that is, the revelation that God gives us in the Bible), then we have these two questions answered right at the beginning of John. God brought everything into existence and, according to verse 4, he turned dead matter into living matter.

Verses 4 and 5: "In Him was life." What is life? Do we have life in us? Is a chair *life?* Are there different kinds of life? For instance, is there a difference between plant life and animal life? Everyone will say yes to this question. Because this is so, why do most people assume that there is no difference between animal life and human life? What is the difference between animal and human life, or are we just an advanced form of protoplasm?

Are there levels of life below plant life? Most people would consider cells to be a form of life. Are there levels of life above human life? How can we know if there is a life-form higher than we are?

Do we have the same kind of life in us as God has in Himself? Many people believe that God is simply an impersonal force. Is God really personal?

What is life? The opposite of death. What is death? Because there are different kinds of life, are there also different kinds of death? You might tell your friends that the Bible says that there are at least two kinds of life and at least two kinds of death.

"What are these kinds?" someone might ask.

Our answer: "John's gospel answers this very soon—before we finish chapter 6. Let's keep reading."

These questions are meant to make our friends think beyond their own limited ideas of life and death. The answers, at this point in the study, are not important. When you ask these questions, tell them that you don't have all of the answers but that the Bible says that there is more to life and death than what most people believe.

I once saw a religious tract that had a list of events followed by a question. It said that man is born, he grows a little, goes to school, becomes a teenager (tough!), picks a profession, gets married and has children, grows old and retires, and dies. Is that all there is to life?

"And the life was the light of men." What is light?

The physicists cannot define light! They can only describe its qualities. Sometimes they say it is waves. However, it often acts like particles. From where does light come? The sun? A physicist would say, "Yes, but not always." A physics student once told me about a phenomenon known as "prime," or "original," light, which is light that has no known source. If light doesn't have to come from the sun, then where does it come from? Genesis tells us that God created light before He created the sun. A person might choose to reject the explanation given in Genesis, but the question of "prime" light is still left open.

If we assume that God made the universe and us, then why did He make our physical light source 93 million miles away? He gave us eyes with which to see, but they are useless without light. Why didn't He place a light source within each of us, like fireflies. We'll answer this question in John 11.

Coming back to our text, what does the *light of men* mean? Is this light the physical light of the sun, or does *light* refer to something else? What? Does this light come *from* men or is this light *for* men? Since the "life" is speaking of the Word, we can safely assume that this light is for men.

Why do people need light? If you entered a dark room, and you had never been in the room before, why would you turn on the light? You would want to see what was in the room; if you had no light, you might run into a table and hurt yourself. Likewise, if we cannot recognize reality and if we can't tell the difference between what is real and what is unreal, we could get hurt in more ways than one.

People also use light to show them the right path, to guide them through the darkness, so they won't stumble along the way. Does the physical aspect of wandering around in darkness have a parallel in the spiritual realm? Do people need a guiding "light" through this world of meaningless darkness to give them meaning and purpose and a goal along life's path so they won't stumble and irrevocably hurt themselves? (Could God have put the sun 93 million miles away from us as an example for us spiritually, that our spiritual light source—which shows us how to live properly—has to come from outside of ourselves rather than from inside (i.e., our own reason or feelings)? From where do most people get meaning in life? Money, power, humanitarianism, good deeds, friends, or happiness? How many people do you know who claim to get their meaning in life solely from God? Is this possible? Where are you going in life? In the next life?

What things do people need to see? The answer lies in verse 5. Where does this light shine? In the darkness. Can we see any parallel between *for men* and *in the darkness*? What is mankind? Is he just body and soul, or is he more—body, soul, and spirit? Is there a difference between mankind's soul and his spirit? We could say that there is no difference, but if there was, what would the difference be? Is mankind's nature basically good? If so, how do we explain the past five thousand years of constant wars? Is mankind completely evil? If so, why does he seem to do good deeds at times? By what measurement do we say that some of a person's deeds are good? What is God's assessment of a person's nature and so-called "good deeds"?

The last half of verse 5 presents us with two options. Either the darkness did not comprehend or understand the light, or the darkness did not overcome or overpower the light. What could these mean? We normally think of light and darkness as inanimate states, but *understanding* and *overpowering* speak of personality. How can inanimate darkness comprehend or overcome something else? Why would darkness want to overcome (overpower, destroy) the light? Did the darkness succeed? What compatibility is there between light and darkness?

Could it be that when people come into contact with the life of the Word (God) this illuminates them? Let's keep this thought in mind as we read the next few verses.

The main ideas to point out in verses 1-5 are as follows.

1.   The Bible teaches that God is personal, not an impersonal

force, that He has a message for all, and that the message is Himself.

2. God made everything; He brought the material into existence and made living matter out of dead matter.
3. Each person needs light to see. There are two kinds of light: the physical sun for physical seeing and an inner light for seeing deeper things.
4. Darkness, as portrayed in the Bible, is more than an inanimate condition. It is more than an absence of light. There seems to be a parallel between man and darkness. We have asked the question, "What is man by nature?"

John 1:6–8

⁶There came a man, sent from God, whose name was John.

⁷He came for a witness, that he might bear witness of the light, that all might believe through him.

⁸He was not the light, but came that he might bear witness of the light.

Verse 6: Is there a contrast between verse 1 and verse 6? Yes, the Word was God, but John was just a man. Which John is being spoken of here? See verses 19-28.

Verses 7 and 8: Why did John come? He came for a witness. What does a witness do? He tells about what he has personally experienced. What had John personally experienced? He had experienced the light. What can that mean? What kind of experience did John have that motivated him to preach and to baptize? Was he just a religious fanatic who thought that he had seen a vision and wanted to propagate his own weird form of religion to everyone at that time?

Why did John bear witness to the light? So that all might believe through him. What does the word *believe* mean? Are there different levels of belief? Can people believe something with their mind and yet not let it affect their actions or lifestyle? Is there such a thing as a belief that changes your life? What is the difference between believing that two and two equals four and believing that the world will end tomorrow? What is the difference between believing that the human being lives on after death and believing that there is no life after death? How will these two beliefs affect our lives before we die?

What is the difference between "blind faith" and "convinced faith"? Does evidence play a part in either one of these? Which one and why? "Blind faith" requires no facts or witnesses. "Blind faith" simply requires blind obedience; no thinking or reasoning is required. People with "blind" faith have sent their brains out to lunch when it comes to their religion. They have and need no facts. They simply believe what they are told or taught by their religious leaders. Back in the 1970s, the religious leaders within the Children of God sect used to require their new converts to chant the following rhyme hundreds of times over and over:

> "If you think, think, think,
> then you stink, stink, stink."

John was obviously not referring to "blind faith" because he came as a witness. He wanted the people to examine and evaluate the facts of his witness. He wanted people to use their brains. He did not demand blind obedience but a reasoning that led to a well-thought-out faith.

We will learn more about belief in verse 12. For now, we simply want to establish that the word *belief* has a wide range of definitions and at least two completely different meanings: believing something mentally and believing something wholeheartedly (being convinced about something).

Did John come in his own authority, or was he representing someone else? Who? Why does the author make a point of saying that John the Baptist was not the light?

The main ideas to point out in verses 6–8 include the following.

1. There is a big difference between "blind faith" and "convinced faith." John the Baptist did not preach "blind faith" because he came as a witness. "Blind faith" requires no witness, no light, and no thinking.

2. A person from God does not represent himself or speak for himself; neither does he stand between God and other people. He simply stands to the side and shows people the way to God.

John 1:9–13

⁹There was the true light which, coming into the world, enlightens every man.

¹⁰He was in the world, and the world was made through Him, and the world did not know Him.

¹¹He came to His own, and those who were His own did not receive Him.

¹²But as many as received Him, to them He gave the right to become children of God, even to those who believe in His name,

¹³who were born not of blood, nor of the will of the flesh, nor of the will of man, but of God.

Verse 9: Why does John emphasize the word *true*? Why didn't John say that "there was *a* true light" or "one of a number of true lights" instead of "the true light"? What is the opposite of true?

These questions should be used to point out the "narrowness" of true Christianity. The answers that our friends give to these questions should not deter us from the text. If you get off onto a discussion of other religions as possible ways to God, just remind them that you did not write the Bible and that they do not have to accept it just because you do. Your (and your friends') primary purpose is to read the Bible to find out what it has to say for itself. If it turns out to be narrower than their own beliefs, then they simply have to choose between what they find comfortable to believe and what is written in the Bible. Stress that you are not "reading anything into the text" of the Bible. You are simply reading it as it stands.

In the first stages of an evangelistic Bible study, I have found it important to stay in John and not to jump around to other cross-references. This gives good continuity to the study and shows our friends how highly we value the context of a passage in our reading. Looking up cross-references can make our friends think that we are pulling verses out of context to support our view of what the Bible says, that we are "interpreting" the Bible to suit ourselves.

The opposite also is true. Cross-references can be very valuable, if they are well placed. Invariably, the question will arise, "What about the other religions? Is Jesus the only way to God?" When it does, and if you wish to break this cardinal rule of not jumping around from text to text, be sure to say something such as, "The Bible has more to say about this subject, but we want to be careful that we don't pull any verses out of their contexts just to support our own viewpoints. I'll show you a couple, but you should not take my word for it. Read the whole passage yourself to see if I have misrepresented what these verses say."

Then point out that Jesus made some very strong claims about Himself and that true Christianity is much narrower than most people want to admit. Without jumping around too much, you might suggest that they read John 14:6 and ask them if that doesn't sound rather narrow to them. Read Matthew 7:13-14 and 7:21-23. You could point out the fact that these are "religious" people. Atheists do not go around saying "Lord, Lord" in this way. Jesus is, in fact, speaking of people who claim to be "Christians" because they are doing things "in My name," not "in God's name." All religions do things in the name of their gods, but only "Christendom" does things in the name of Jesus. Point out what these people actually did in Jesus' name in Matthew 7. If a person can't get into heaven on the basis of such good deeds as these, then how can he get there?

Now, back at John 1:9 we must ask what this true light does. He enlightens every man. How many people are enlightened? Only those in the West? Only those who have Bibles? How can a person be enlightened if he has never seen a Bible or spoken to someone who has? What about the natives in Africa who have never heard? Your friends will inevitably raise this question sometime, so you should raise it for them. It will show them that you already know their questions and have dealt with them to some degree. The answer to this question is given very clearly in Romans 1, but we don't want to take on Romans before we have finished with John!

Continuing in the text, what does *enlightened* mean? "To come to understand something." How much does one have to understand, before one is considered enlightened? Does being enlightened mean that everyone will go to heaven? Can a person be enlightened about something and still reject what he or she has come to understand?

This question is very important. Is the Bible saying here that every person has received some knowledge and some understanding of this knowledge from God, even if we are not told in this passage how each person has been enlightened?

Don't get hung up on their demand for answers to all of these questions. Most of the answers are found in the first few chapters of John. Tell them to have patience, that you are asking questions to encourage more in-depth thinking, and to keep reading.

For your own study of the Word, you might ask these questions about enlightenment in Hebrews 6:4-6.

Verse 10: The world did not know Him. Was it an accident that the world didn't know Him? Was it intentional? The text does not say at this point. Maybe the world was out having a picnic and just missed the true light accidentally. Maybe the world regrets this oversight deeply. Maybe the world doesn't even know that it missed the true light. Verse 11 might give us more insight into the subject.

Verse 11: Who were His own? (Probably the Jews, but so far the passage has been talking about humankind in general.) Did they actively reject Him, or was it all a big mistake? Remember verses 5 and 10: "The darkness did not understand (or overpower) it" and "the world did not receive Him." The verb phrase *did not receive* is active. It would seem that the world could not have cared less about the true light and has actively rejected Him.

Verse 12: This verse contains enough discussion for an entire evening! You will probably spend more time on this verse than all of the rest of chapter 1, and you will come back to it repeatedly throughout your study of John. Therefore, I have included a number of examples to illustrate this verse. You will probably need to review its content and repeat these and other illustrations numerous times with your unsaved friends. The key to learning and grasping new concepts is repetition, so do not tire of going over this and similar verses numerous times. Your patience will probably lead to the salvation of your friends.

At this point, after raising so many questions from the last verses, I usually break the train of thought with a completely different question.

Is every person a child of God? Almost everyone will answer, "Yes." Their reasoning is that because God made everyone, then we are automatically his children. If they say no, then just go on with your questions.

How does the Bible answer this question? Read verse 12 again. After you have established the fact that there are two classes of people (children of God and everyone else), ask, "If everyone is not a child of God, then what are they?" We are all His creatures, but we are not all members of His family. According to verse 4, we have all been created by God, but it does not say that we are all children of God. Regardless of what many different religions say, the Bible does not teach that everyone is a child of God.

How does one become a child of God? Give your unsaved friends time to answer this question (common responses are by baptism, confirmation, and church membership). By receiving and believing. Is it a fair assumption that a person must understand what these two words *receiving* and *believing* mean or that person cannot become a child of God? Emphasize this!

How do we receive a person? What does it mean to believe in someone? I once heard the story about a man who had a rope stretched across Niagara Falls, and then he advertised that he was going to walk across the rope. On the day he was to do this, he asked a number of people if they believed that he could do it. Naturally, they all said yes. Then he asked if they believed that he could do it carrying a large oil drum on his shoulders. Most of them said no, and then he did it. They all became believers. Then he asked if they believed that he could carry a person across on his shoulders. Everyone said yes; they believed that he could do it. Then he went from person to person, asking each of them if they would be willing to be carried across. No one said yes—except a small boy. The man did not carry anyone across (the boy's mother wouldn't let him). Everyone "believed" that he could do it, but no one trusted him enough to climb onto his shoulders. Everyone could say that they "knew" he could do it, but no one really "believed in him" enough to entrust their life to him. Becoming a child of God requires this trust or "believing in" the Lord Jesus.

To believe in someone's name means the same thing. When an ambassador is put in charge of an embassy in a foreign country, he is representing his king or president. He is acting "in the name of the president." He trusts that his president knows best, and he has chosen to align himself with the president's views and goals. His own safety often depends upon the president's decisions. In real life, no ambassador would completely trust the views of a president, even though he might have to abide by them. That president would have to be perfect. In our study of

John, we need to keep before us the question "Is Jesus perfect?" What does Jesus say about Himself? (He made some incredible statements about Himself, as we will see in our study of John 5.) What did others say about Him? Who told the truth? Who lied? Why? We will answer all of these questions before we have finished John.

When we put our trust in another person, the most important question becomes whether that person is trustworthy. We might have given ourselves to this person completely in blind faith, but our trust would be useless if the object of our trust was not dependable. We see this every day in the news when we hear about thousands of religious fanatics killing hundreds of people "in the name of" their religious leader. Jesus spoke about this type of blind faith in John 15 and 16. We will come to that later.

When we use the word *believe,* we always use it with an object. If we heard someone say, "I believe," we would quite naturally ask, "What or whom do you believe?" If your friend says to you, "I have my belief. That's good enough for me," you might ask him, "But is your belief good enough for God?" Or you might give him an illustration. Suppose that I have a cup of boiling water in front of me. What would you think if I said, "I believe that if I stick my finger in this cup of hot water, I'll burn my finger. On the basis of this 'belief,' I am going to heaven."

That is obviously absurd. It points out, however, that not just any belief is good enough to get a person into heaven. If I wanted to travel abroad, I would need a passport. Imagine if I arrived at a border and gave the border guard my passport, which was twenty years out of date. I could yell all day long that the passport was good enough to get me through the border, but I might end up in a foreign jail.

What passport does God require to get into heaven? After all, heaven belongs to Him. Doesn't He have the right to determine what is needed to get into it? Doesn't He have the right to reject anyone who doesn't meet up to His standards? Some people say, "I'm just as good as the next person. If that person gets into heaven, then I will, too." Doesn't this assume that God has to accept our standards for living and for entering heaven? What if God does not agree with our views? Who is going to judge whom after we die?

Do you know if you are a child of God? How can you know?

Verse 13: What does a person have to do to take part in human society? He has to be born a physical human being. What does a person have to do to take part in God's society? Doesn't he have to be born on a different plane, on a spiritual level (i.e., be born again)? Does being born physically make you a child of God? (Have you ever met anyone who wasn't born physically?) How can a person be born a child of God?

What does it mean to be a member of a family? Can my son ever stop being my son? Even if he disowns me? Does this mean that not everyone can say that God is their Father? What do we think of when we hear the word *father*? If a person is not "born of God," what name can they call God? (They can call Him "Creator" but not "Father.")

How are the following three phrases different: "born not of blood, nor of the will of the flesh, nor of the will of man"? Can a person get to heaven by inheritance, that is, his parents are believers and their bloodline qualifies their children for heaven? Can a person get to heaven by doing good works (i.e., works of the flesh)? Can a person get to heaven because some priest sprinkles water over him and *says* that he is a child of God, by the will of man?

The main ideas to be brought out in verses 9–13 are:

1. All are enlightened (i.e., have been given some information about God).
2. According to verse 11, most people seem to have rejected God.
3. Not everyone is a child of God. Just as a person has to be born physically to take part in human society, so does a person have to be born spiritually to take part in God's society.

4. Being born of God cannot be accomplished by any natural human means; it has to be done by God.
5. God's requirements for being born spiritually are very simple: placing our trust solely in Jesus Christ to save us.

John 1:14-18

[14]And the Word became flesh, and dwelt among us, and we beheld His glory, glory as of the only begotten from the Father, full of grace and truth.

[15]John bore witness of Him, and cried out, saying, "This was He of whom I said, 'He who comes after me has a higher rank than I, for He existed before me.'"

[16]For of His fullness we have all received, and grace upon grace.

[17]For the law was given through Moses; grace and truth were realized through Jesus Christ.

[18]No man has seen God at any time; the only begotten God, who is in the bosom of the Father, He has explained Him.

Remember: None of these questions is meant to be answered on the spot but merely to spark a good discussion. The principles will be brought out at the end of the questions.

Verse 14: All religions speak of humanity's trying to reach God. The process starts within each person. How effective is this? Let's take an example.

Imagine that I am sitting in a living room, and over in the corner I see an ant. Suppose that this ant wants to communicate with me. What should he do? Should he come over, crawl up on my shoe, and yell at me in ant language? But what if I don't want to talk to him? I could leave the house, and the ant would never have the chance to reach me. So before the ant can speak with me, I have to want to speak with the ant. Could we possibly find God if He didn't want to speak with us? Doesn't it make logical sense that God would have to take the initiative in communicating with us before we could communicate with Him?

Suppose that I wanted to speak with the ant. How would I do it? I could go over to the ant and talk to him, but he wouldn't understand. I would have to speak "ant language" to him. I would have to describe myself in terms that the ant would understand. Because I am far more complicated than the ant, I would have to describe myself very simply. If an ant wanted to get to know me, then everything would depend on me for this to take place.

However, the best way to communicate with that ant, would be to become an ant! Great idea, but it could be dangerous. There are millions of ants in the world. What if they didn't like me? They could even crucify (oops!), uh, kill me! How has God chosen to communicate with us? What does verse 14 say?

Religion is humanity's attempt to reach God; the direction goes from us to God. The Bible is the only religious book that turns the process around and starts with God. As we can see in verse 14, humanity did not reach out to God first, but God reached out to humanity by becoming one of us.

What does it mean to "behold someone's glory?" Do we normally speak of another person in this way?

You might explain the term *only begotten*. It does not refer to time but to priority. The same term is used in Hebrews in referring to Isaac as Abraham's "only-begotten son." This term cannot refer to time because Ishmael was Abraham's first child.

Normally, for our unsaved friends, I simply ask them what it means, and they usually say, "The only son." Rather than going into a complicated explanation of the Greek text, along with the extensive apparatus in the footnotes relating what Lange and Calvin and Joe Bloggs say about this word, it would probably be best to keep the explanation as simple as possible.

What are grace and truth? If your friends have trouble explaining these terms, give them an example from a law court. If we commit a crime and have to go to court for it, what do we hope the judge will do? Show us grace, of course—that is, overlook our bad deed. The last thing we want is the truth! What do we want if we are innocent? Would we be interested in grace? No, what we want is the truth. In any case, we seldom see the two terms, *grace* and *truth,* together in the same context. We need to discuss each term separately first.

How would you define *grace*? Get everyone's opinion on this question, then look it up in a dictionary. Grace is undeserved and unearned favor, in spite of earned punishment. Many examples come to mind. A teacher gives a student a better grade than that student has earned. A judge is lenient with a criminal and gives him a reprimand instead of a jail sentence. Think of some other examples from your own family life or school or work experiences.

You should have some interesting discussions about the concept of truth. Is there only one kind of truth? If not, how many different kinds are there? Into what definite categories can we classify truth? Truth can be absolute or relative. Everybody has their own view of what is true. Over the centuries, philosophers have written much on the concept of relative truth. Many have come to the same conclusion: All truth is relative.

And yet, within a given system, some truths are absolute. For example, if you jumped out of a fifth-floor window, you would fall down, not up. You might experiment by throwing a small rock out of the window a thousand times. Each time it would fall down, not up. You would probably assume that if you jumped out, you would fall down, not up. If you try to violate this truth, you are in for a real shock. Jumping out of the window proves that you have not appreciated the gravity of the situation!

We humans cannot violate a truth just because it does not appeal to us. We learn this in the physical world as we grow up, and we know it intuitively as adults. Does the same hold true in the moral world? Are there moral truths that will produce automatically negative results if we violate them? Can we make any truth relative, as it pleases us, without expecting consequences?

What if you are faced with two systems of relative truth? How do you choose the right one? Is there a right one? Can they both be right at the same time?

Let me give an example. Assume that you are a student and you have to take a test. Your teacher returns the test to you, and he has written across it, "Failed." You ask him why you failed the test, and he says, "You got only 15 percent of the answers correct. You needed 70 percent correct to pass." What if you told him that he had to give you a passing grade because your grading scale requires that you get only 10 percent correct. Because you got 15 percent right, you deserve a passing grade. What would the teacher say to you? If he did anything but laugh at you, he might politely point out that his grading system was the "right" one to be taken into consideration for this test. After all, the teacher made the test. It was the teacher's **test,** not the student's.

Does God have a grading system? Is it relative or absolute? What if we find our moral values conflicting with God's moral values? Who would be right? Do we believe that we can talk God out of His views and make Him change His mind to agree with our way of seeing things? What if we can't? What if God's "truth" is absolute and does not fit into our relative way of thinking (i.e., that we can't change a rule to suit our whims)?

What if God's laws are too high for us to reach? What if God requires us to be perfect, as He is?

Can you imagine what heaven is like? Do you think that everything and everybody will be perfect in heaven? If so, are you perfect? If heaven is perfect but you are not, then if God let you into heaven, it wouldn't be perfect anymore! Why should God let imperfect you into His perfect heaven?

(What our unsaved friends do not realize, as you ask them all of these questions, is that God does require perfection to get into heaven and that the human being, on his own merit, cannot meet God's standards. This is the very reason we need the death of Christ to pay our debt of sin and the resurrection of Christ to raise us with Him in glory. The Lord Jesus does not come alongside and help us get into heaven. He buys us with His blood and takes us by pure grace with Him there.)

These questions are designed to get our friends to think about their own relative views of truth and to question whether their views might be different from God's. We especially want them to think about the consequences of holding views different from those of God.

Eventually, you must ask, "If the Bible is God's Word, and you discover something in the Bible with which you disagree, what will be your reaction? The normal reaction will be to reject the Bible as God's Word, but what if you're wrong? It doesn't seem very safe or clever to disagree with God. What do you think?"

Although we seldom hear grace and truth referred to in the same context, we cannot have grace without a standard by which to measure it. A judge cannot show grace without a standard of judgment by which to determine why a person has not deserved this grace. There must be a rule or law that has been broken that requires a judgment before grace, rather than punishment, can be given. What standard of judgment or truth does God use to measure whether we have earned heaven? Why should God show us grace? On what basis have we "earned his grace" (a contradiction in terms)?

At this point, you might end the discussion with the concept of a person earning his way into heaven. The following questions might help you with the discussion.

Some people think that they can earn their way into heaven. I think that idea demonstrates how incredibly proud human beings can be. Most people who believe this usually have their own scale in mind. When they die, they hope that their good deeds will outweigh their bad deeds so they can go to heaven. If not, they assume that they will spend some time between heaven and earth, suffering somehow, to pay for their overabundance of bad deeds. Then they think that they will be allowed into heaven. If the scale shows only bad deeds, they assume that this person will go to hell.

Everyone asks, in effect, "How many good deeds do I need to get into heaven?"

What I find interesting is that no one ever asks, "How few bad deeds are allowed before entrance into heaven is barred?" What if God does not allow *any* bad deeds in this life? What if the scale has to be tilted completely toward the side of *good* deeds? How can someone believe that he could live a life "good enough" for God? How can a person believe that he can do *anything* good enough for God? Are we saying that God has to accept our puny efforts at perfection just because we can't do any better? How good is God compared with us?

I've heard people say, "If that person gets into heaven then I'll make it, too. I'm just as good as he is." What if God's standards are not our standards? An unsaved young man once said to the late Dr. John Mitchell, "If you get into heaven, then I will, too. I'm just as good as you are." Dr. Mitchell sadly replied, "What a rotten standard of measurement you are using!"

If a person has to meet God's standard of perfection, then who can get into heaven? Only someone who is perfect. Could a person be a sinner in this life and yet God see him as perfect and let him into heaven? What would it take to make God look at you and declare you to be perfect?

If we keep reading long enough, we will get the answers to these questions in John's gospel.

What does "full of" grace and truth mean? How can one person be full of both of these virtues? If a person is full of grace, it would probably mean that he is constantly overlooking the faults of others, in which case, he can't be full of truth, or he would always be telling people the truth about themselves! Not a pleasant person to have around. Do you know anyone who is constantly overlooking the faults of others? Neither do I.

Maybe "full of truth" means that he is always being truthful. Do you know anyone who never tells a lie? Do you lie? Admit it. We all do at times. We usually justify it by describing the color of the lie: "It was just a little white lie."

If we can't think of anyone who is "full of grace" and "full of truth," to whom could John be referring in this verse? Certainly not to just a normal human being! What else does John say about this person?

Verse 15: Point out the apparent contradictions in this verse. How can a person come after someone and still have existed beforehand? Of whom is John talking? Until now, we still have not read any name for the person who is being described. We won't find a name until we come to verse 17.

Verse 16: What is meant by His "fullness?" What have all received? Most people have not given much thought to the things that they receive each day. They take for granted the air that they breathe. They assume that the bread on their table was put there by their own hard labor. I once asked an unsaved friend, "Why should God give you one more breath of air to breathe? Why should God let you live one more second? Have you earned that next breath of air? Have you earned the life you have?"

What does "grace upon grace" mean? Can a person be given too much grace? Can a person be given enough grace?

Verse 17: Of what law is John speaking? Who was Moses? Don't go into extreme detail with the answers to these questions, giving an overview of the Old Testament. A detailed answer will come later.

What is the difference between "given through" and "were realized"? This answer could be significant, as we compare Moses with Jesus later in John's gospel.

Verse 18: This verse brings together the ideas that John has expressed so far. God revealed Himself to man by becoming a human being. Most people have rejected Him. Some have accepted Him and have thereby become children of God. In any case, Jesus Christ, the God-Man, has come to show us what God is like.

If you wanted to know what your neighbor was like, and you did not want to ask him, whom would you ask about him? You could ask the milkman what he was like. He might tell you that your neighbor drinks three quarts of milk a week, but this information will not do a lot of good in really getting to know your neighbor. You might ask the mailman and learn that your neighbor writes and receives few letters. You might deduce from this information that your neighbor is lonely, but you cannot be sure. You might ask his boss or one of his employees, but you are still stuck with not really knowing your neighbor. Your best choice would be to speak with his wife or children. They would be considered the "closest" to him.

What comes to mind when you hear the words *in the bosom of*? Closeness? Unity? Love? Attachment? Intimate knowledge? Most people think of a happy little baby, resting against his mother's bosom. Can you see why John uses this phrase to describe the relationship between the Father and the Son? The unique, special, close, intimate relationship could not be expressed better. Who else would know better what God was like if not God's very own Son, with whom He has lived from all eternity past?

What is John really claiming about Jesus? Let's go back to our example of getting to know our neighbor. Apart from meeting him personally and developing a relationship directly, we are limited to speaking with others about him. Jesus goes beyond just saying that He wanted to tell us *about* God. He claims to show us *God*.

If someone came to your home and said that they had a message for you from God, you might laugh and not take that person seriously. If he came, however, and claimed that he was going to show you God, you might become concerned for his mental health. If he were serious, you might ask him to prove that he was close enough to God to be able to show you what God was like. That would require miracles of all kinds.

The problem we face here is what kind of "evidence" we are willing to accept as proof. As we read further in John, this problem will confront us repeatedly. Jesus performs miracle after miracle, but the people do not accept his miracles as evidence of his credibility.

For your own benefit, compare the following passages of Scripture.

John 5. Jesus healed a man, but the Pharisees would not consider this act to be a miracle because Jesus had done it on the Sabbath, which broke one of their religious laws. The Lord never broke a law from the Old Testament, nor did He break any civil laws.

John 6. The Lord multiplied the bread and the fish, and on the next day, the people asked Him for a sign (v. 30).

John 8 and 9. The Pharisees admitted their own sinfulness in 8:9, and the Lord claimed sinless perfection for Himself by challenging them to show Him where He had sinned (8:46). In 9:24, the Pharisees claimed to know that Jesus was a sinner, even though they could not point out to Him even one sin that He had committed.

John 10. Although Jesus had done numerous works by this time, most of the people still did not believe that He came from God. He confronted the issue directly, saying, "If I do not do the works of My Father, do not believe Me; but if I do them, though you do not believe Me, believe the works, that you may know and understand that the Father is in Me, and I in the Father" (10:37–38). At this point, the Jews wanted to kill Him because they clearly understood what the Lord Jesus was claiming. He was claiming to be God (see 10:33).

He also spoke to them in figurative language (10:6), but no one understood what He meant. In spite of this lack of understanding, the people reacted in two ways. Some of them said that He was possessed by a demon, and others accepted what He was saying. Those who accepted Him did so because Jesus had performed a miracle by giving a blind man his sight. Miracles demonstrate credibility, but miracles are useless if a person willfully hangs on to his or her own preconceived ideas and is not willing to accept factual evidence.

John 11. Here Jesus performed the greatest miracle of all. He raised a man from the dead. He received the same two reactions. "Many therefore of the Jews, who had come to Mary and beheld what He had done, believed in Him. But some of them went away to the Pharisees, and told them the things which Jesus had done" (11:45–46).

Do not show your unsaved friends all of these verses while you are still in chapter 1. I have included them here so that you can see what you are going to have to communicate (through questions!) over and over to your friends. *Willingness* to accept factual evidence for belief (not blind faith) will be the deciding factor in your friends' lives.

We want to keep the questions and discussion of this verse simple for our unsaved friends, so we do not get bogged down in a theological discussion of whether it is possible to "see" God.

Exodus 33:11 tells us that "the Lord used to speak to Moses face to face, just as a man speaks to his friend." In Exodus 33:20, God told Moses, "You cannot see My face, for no man can see Me and live!" Either we choose to see a direct contradiction here, or we understand that God is using the simile in verse 11, "just as a man speaks to his friend," to explain what He meant by the words *face to face*.

Some translations will say "the only begotten son," and others will say "the only begotten God." Why would this difference exist? (Some scribes knew that Jesus was God and simply wrote *God* instead of *Son*. They thought that they were clarifying things for the reader.)

If a person wanted to get to know God, what would that person have to do, according to this verse? If Jesus "explains" God, then we would have to go to Jesus to find out what God is like. If God has become the person of Jesus Christ, we might want to ask ourselves why He did so. Why didn't He become a plant or an animal? Why didn't He become an angel? Why did He choose to become a human being? That would seem the best way to communicate with us. He could actually show us, in His human form, what He, God, is really like. And He could show us in terms that we can understand.

I would find it hard to identify with an angel because I'm not one, and I've never talked with one or even seen one. And I do not believe that God is less than man, so I probably would not listen to a dog if he spoke to me and told me that he was God. Would you?

Some key questions to ask our unsaved friends are: "What does God look like (not His physical form) as portrayed by

Jesus? Does this picture of God match my own preconceived views of how God should be? What if God is different from whatever I have imagined Him to be? If Jesus is God, and if His portrayal of God is correct, should my picture of God change, or should I demand that God change to fit my picture of how I think He should be?"

Whichever questions you use, remember to keep the conversation simple so that your friends do not miss the main point: Jesus came to show us God, not just to tell us something about Him.

The main ideas in verses 14-18 are as follows.

1. God initiated the process of reaching out to us by becoming a man.
2. Although grace and truth are usually considered opposites, we need both of them to live in this world.
3. Relative and absolute truths are distinctly different.
4. What does God require before He will let a person into His heaven? Discuss the concept of "good works" and "perfection."
5. Where do we get everything we take for granted (such as the air or the sun)?
6. Contrast Moses with Jesus. Keep it simple.
7. God has chosen to become a man to show us what He, God, is really like.
8. Are we willing to accept Him as He is? Or do we want to hang onto our own ideas of how we want God to be? Are we demanding that God change Himself to suit us so that we can remain comfortable in our views?

As with all of the other main points, keep these points simple and direct. You are not interested in having your unsaved friends understand everything in the text the first time through. I have read through the gospel of John numerous times and almost every time I see something new.

The questions and answers from John 1:1-18 should give you enough material to get you through the first one or two Bible studies with your friends. As you continue in the study, begin to form your own questions from the text. It should get easier as you go along. From this point, I will remark on only the main ideas that should be emphasized in each passage and on the verses that have played a central part in my ministry of evangelism.

John 1:19–28

Why did the Pharisees want to know who John the Baptist was? The Pharisees believed that they represented God and the only way to God. John's ministry was threatening because it challenged their position of authority and power. He had begun to baptize hundreds of people; simultaneously, he rejected the leadership of the Pharisees. John had not gone through the proper channels (i.e., Pharisee Bible School). He did not have the appropriate religious credentials to represent God.

How does one receive God's authority? How does one receive human authority? How can we tell the difference?

John 1:29

This verse could take an hour to discuss. Don't be in a hurry to get through it. Let people express their views.

What is sin? Discuss this topic at length. Who has the right to define what is and is not a sin? What standard of measurement should a person use to determine if something is a sin? We all admit that no one is perfect, but what makes us imperfect? Who says that we're not perfect? Some people are better than others, but when we say this, we are measuring ourselves on a relative scale. Why don't we compare ourselves with God? What does God think of our relative standards of perfection? If God calls something a sin but we do not, who is right? Who has the right to say that something is sin, even when we disagree with them? When we have finished this life, will God judge us on the basis of our relative standards or His absolute standards?

What purposes do lambs have in different religions? Sacrifices and scapegoats. Worshipers would sacrifice a lamb to appease God. Appeasing God meant satisfying His anger and thereby keeping Him at a distance. Normally, a lamb would be sacrificed to keep God away. What about the lamb *of God*? Why would God provide the lamb for the sacrifice? The answer to this question is clearly spelled out in Romans 3:26, but we will not jump into Romans until we are finished with John.

What are human requirements for taking away sin? What are God's requirements for taking away sin? Is God obligated to accept our requirements, or must we accept His? Is there a difference between covering over sin and taking it away?

John 1:30–51

Nathanael was a skeptic. He went with Phillip, but his mind was already made up. Nothing good could come out of Nazareth.

When he arrived, Jesus told Nathanael two things about himself. Having never met Nathanael personally, Jesus claimed to be able to read Nathanael's heart, "Behold, an Israelite indeed, in whom is no guile!" Nathanael responded quite naturally: "How do you know me?" As everyone knows, only God can read a person's character without a previous relationship. Nathanael was still not convinced that Jesus was the Messiah. It would take a lot of persuading to convince him that Jesus could see Nathanael's innermost being.

To confirm His ability to see people as they really are, Jesus told Nathanael that He had seen him under the fig tree. Apparently, the fig tree was far enough away for this to have been physically impossible. Why do I say this? Look at Nathanael's reaction. If the fig tree had been only a few yards away, Nathanael would have simply laughed at Jesus. On the basis of Jesus' statement (that he could see beyond the physical limitations of nature), however, Nathanael came to the same conclusion as John the Baptist: "Rabbi, You are the Son of God; You are the King of Israel." Nathanael changed from a skeptic to a devoted follower.

If the Bible is correct in relating this story about Jesus, what are the ramifications for my life? Does Jesus know where I am at all times? Even more important, can He read my heart and see what kind of person I really am, apart from the front that I put on for others? How would you react to meeting a person who could read your thoughts? That person could be dangerous if he did not love you. The Lord Jesus can see right through us. Does He love us? How do these thoughts make you feel? (Discuss!)

John 2:1–12

How did Jesus treat Mary, His mother, at this wedding? Why? How did Mary respond to Jesus' question? This is the only place in the Bible where Mary gave a command. What was commanded here (v. 5)? What type of miracle did Jesus perform? How long does it take to make good wine (a time miracle)? What difference is there between water and wine (a chemical and molecular miracle)? What was the purpose of this miracle (v. 11)? Why didn't Jesus make enough wine for all of the weddings that year? Why didn't He heal all of the sick and the lame in the whole world while He was on the earth? Why did He do any miracles at all?

The next paragraph of questions is important for people who believe that Mary remained a virgin her whole life. Your friends will begin to see that the things "religions" teach do not always agree with the Bible.

What was the difference between Jesus' brothers and His disciples? Why didn't John mention Jesus' cousins instead of His brothers? Who were His brothers (Matt. 13:55)? Did Jesus have any sisters (Matt. 13:56)? How many? What does the word *until* in Matthew 1:25 mean? (It means that Joseph finally got his honeymoon!)

John 2:13–25

Does this story match the typical view of a quiet, soft-spoken, humble Jesus? Did Jesus have the right to clean out the temple? Why or why not? What would Jesus say about our religions today? What would He want to clean out?

How do verses 24 and 25 relate to what Jesus told Nathanael? What did John mean when he wrote that Jesus knew what was in man?

John 3:1–36

The main ideas in this chapter relate to pride. Nicodemus prided himself on being a teacher of Israel, a true representative of God. Jesus attacked him at his strongest point by pointing out that Nicodemus did not even know the answer to the most important and most basic question of life: How can a person get into heaven? If a theologian does not have the correct answer to this question, then his theological training is a hypocritical waste. Verse 11 reveals the main problem: "You do not receive our witness." They did not want to believe. The chapter ends (v. 36) by equating belief with obedience. The Father will not accept as legitimate a belief that does not result in obedience to Christ.

John 4:1–54

The woman at the well had a different problem: morality. The Lord Jesus did not attack her as He did Nicodemus but pointed out quite clearly that her life was not in order. "You have well said, 'I have no husband'; for you have had five husbands; and the one whom you now have is not your husband." A good question to ask would be, "What was Jesus' opinion of this woman's moral lifestyle?"

As chapter 3 ended by defining faith as obedience, chapter 4 shows us that our morals will also have to conform to the will of Christ. Intellectual belief is useless without the corresponding evidence of a lifestyle change, and this must often occur in our moral values. Remember, Jesus rejected the moral sin of the woman, but He did not reject the woman.

John 5:1–47

If you get this far in your study with your unsaved friends, then they are on the way to becoming believers. The claims made by Jesus in this chapter will leave them with only one of two options.

In verse 18, John tells us that the Jews wanted to kill Jesus because He claimed to be equal with God. According to the Old Testament, if people claimed equality with God, they were committing blasphemy against God and were to be stoned. Jesus claimed to be able to give life, "just as the Father raises the dead." Jesus was claiming the same creative power as God Himself (v. 21). He claimed the right to choose who should receive this life (v. 21). He claimed the right to judge all men (v. 22). He demanded that all men "honor [worship] the Son, even as they honor [worship] the Father" (v. 23).

The culmination is in verse 24, where Jesus equated hearing (obeying) His word with believing the Father, which frees a person from being judged. Most people believe that everyone will be judged for their works, and if they have done "enough" good, then they will go to heaven. Jesus tells us here that we can have eternal life *now,* and miss the judgment altogether.

These claims leave us with only one of three options. How would you react if someone you had not met before announced that He was equal with God, that He could create life the same way God does, that He would judge everyone, that He demanded the same worship given to God, and that obeying His Word was equal to believing God? Jesus either needed to be treated for severe psychological problems, was deliberately lying, or was and is God. His claims leave us with no other alternatives.

Jesus again stated the main problem in verse 40: "You are unwilling to come to Me, that you may have life."

John 6:1–71

One of the main thoughts of this chapter is found in verses 28 and 29. The Jews, as is the case in most religions, held a theology of good works to get into heaven. "What shall we do, that we may work the works of God?" Jesus corrected this false view, saying, "This is the work of God, that you believe in Him whom He has sent."

In the feeding of the five thousand and the following teaching about His body and blood, the Lord Jesus equated eating His body and drinking His blood with believing in Him. Compare verse 47 with verse 51, both of which result in the same thing: eternal life.

Eating is a natural illustration for believing. We eat food for two reasons: to stay alive physically and for pleasure. One person eats to live; the other person lives to eat. A person believes for the same reasons: to stay alive eternally and for the joy of knowing God personally.

The processes are the same as well. No one eats by putting food on his head or gluing it to his skin. To receive the proper benefit from eating, we must put the food inside of us and let it work from the inside out. If we do not eat properly, food is useless to us, and we could die. Believing functions the same way. True belief is not outward religion, in which a person puts on a spiritual mask. True belief consists of giving our lives over to Christ and trusting Him, through our obedience, to change our heart's attitude toward sin in our lives.

The two choices given in chapters 5 and 6 result in one of two reactions. "As a result of this many of His disciples withdrew, and were not walking with Him anymore" (6:66). "Lord, to whom shall we go? You have the words of eternal life" (6:68).

DO IT!

1. Have you started reading John's gospel with an unsaved friend? If not, then *do it!*
2. If you have, does your friend have any friends who might like to join you?
3. If this book has been a help to you, or if you know how I could improve it, please let me know by writing to me at the publisher's address. I am very interested in improving my own evangelistic efforts.

Chapter 16

What to Do Next with New Believers

Beginning the Discipleship Process

When I first named this chapter, my wife objected and said that I should call it "How to Disciple New Believers." My title reminded her of an evangelism conference where I once spoke. During a panel discussion, a good friend was moderating, and he asked me, "What do you do with new believers?"

"Do?" I answered with a grin. "We shoot them. It saves them from persecution and difficulties going through the sanctification process. We just send them straight to heaven."

There was a stunned silence before the audience exploded into laughter. My friend just dropped his head onto the table in embarrassment. He still loves me.

Therefore, I've added the subtitle.

Back to the Basics

God revealed Himself to your unsaved friends through the Bible. The Holy Spirit convicted your friends of sin, and this led to the obedience of faith. Your friends changed kingdoms.

Now, as new members of God's kingdom, your friends want to know and experience everything that the Lord promised for those who choose to love and follow Him. How can you help your friends now? *Stay with the Bible!* Growth in the Christian life occurs through the continued work of the Holy Spirit through the Word of God. Help your friends to establish a habit of Bible reading and prayer, just as you've been doing together these past few weeks or months. New babies need constant care.

If you haven't already invited your friends to church, now is the time to go back to the Bible and think through this next move. Don't be in a hurry. You have taught your friends that the Bible, as God's truth, will help us discern false gospels. Now you want to teach your disciples that the Bible can also point us to a good church. Although no perfect church exists, the Bible gives believers very clear teaching on what a good church will be like. Let's look at God's textbook on the church.

Evangelism

So then, those who had received his word were baptized; and there were added that day about three thousand souls.

—Acts 2:41

On the first day of the church, Peter preached the gospel, and three thousand people accepted his message. The first mark of a New Testament church is leadership that is evangelizing. The believers in a church will follow their leaders, often even subconsciously. A few believers in a church might be witnessing, but if the leaders are not doing so, the church will not be healthy. And bigger problems might exist.

A church will often become ingrown when the leaders stop evangelizing. Eventually, legalism sets in, and legalism leads to a rejection of other groups of believers who differ in just the smallest detail of that church's doctrinal statement. Evangelism keeps believers from having leftover energy for fighting with other believers!

I met Bob at a missionary conference in Vienna, Austria. He was the owner of a chain of large truck stops on the East Coast. He had brought many people to the Lord through evangelistic

Bible studies and had written a book on his method. He was speaking to the missionaries about evangelism. He told them that he would never take a new believer to church for at least two years after initial conversion! He said that many churches are not evangelizing, and he didn't want this poor role modeling to rub off on the new converts. He didn't want them to begin thinking that a lack of evangelism was "normal" for a Christian!

Remember the deacon at the end of chapter 2? Will your unsaved friends feel welcome *and* feel comfortable bringing their unsaved friends?

You want to take your new believers to a church that will encourage evangelism. Look for the following negative and positive indications of this attitude.

Watch for the following negative things:

- constant criticism of other churches;
- leaders claiming that they don't have the gift of evangelism or that they did when they were younger but that they're too tired now;
- programs for believers almost every evening of the week, leaving no time for evangelistic Bible studies; and
- an attitude that spending time with the unsaved will contaminate the believer.

Watch for the following positive things:

- leaders who teach about evangelism, who use examples of their own evangelistic endeavors, and who get excited about any believers who are doing evangelism (like cheerleaders!);
- people talking about their evangelistic successes and failures;
- church programs geared to include the unsaved in friendly times of fun and games (e.g., picnics or parties);
- Bible classes for new believers that often overflow.

Baptism

So then, those who had received his word were baptized; and there were added that day about three thousand souls.

—Acts 2:41

I don't want to write a sermon on the importance of baptism in this book. I will give just one illustration.

Imagine a young man who has no girlfriend. When you ask him if he is interested in getting married some day, he replies, "Oh, I don't need a wife. I have a wedding ring." What would be your response? You might wonder why someone would want the *symbol* of a relationship but not the *relationship* itself. And then the young man tells you that he has one hundred wedding rings, and that they are far better than just one wife. This young man has a serious defect in his thinking.

Now imagine a young man falling in love with a young woman. Eventually, they both declare their feelings for each other and their desire to marry. A few weeks go by, and the young woman finally asks, "So, when am I going to get. . . ?"

"Get what?" he replies.

"You know!" She rolls her eyes to the heavens. "The ring, dummy!"

"The ring?! Why do you need a ring? You have me!"

What would be her response?

A ring declares ownership. My wedding ring tells the world that I am no longer available. I belong to my spouse.

When it comes to baptism, believers make two mistakes. Many confuse reality with symbols. If a person does not have a personal faith in the Lord Jesus, he or she could be baptized one hundred times, and the only result would be a huge waste of water.

Some, however, underestimate the importance of symbols, especially if those symbols have been given by the Lord Jesus! At the very minimum, baptism tells the world to whom the believer belongs. Jesus takes symbols of ownership very seriously.

⚜

Having looked at evangelism and baptism carefully, you might want to go over the following verses with your converts before a final decision is made. Concentrate on the following four essentials. The form of the church is not of major importance. Structures and form might have become encrusted in an older church. Don't get sidetracked into minor issues. Leaders in a good church, however, will have recognized these four items as absolute necessities for a healthy church.

Teaching

And they were continually devoting themselves to the apostles' teaching and to fellowship, to the breaking of bread and to prayer.

—Acts 2:42

Keep your Bible study going with your new converts. Continue through the gospel you are reading. Don't make any abrupt changes. As your friends grow in faith, they will need more than milk on which to feed. This result will come automatically if you continue into the Epistles. You might even consider taking on Romans after you've finished a gospel. Eventually, your friends will start reading the Old Testament and will probably stumble into Hebrews.

Colossians 2:6-7 outlines the continuing process of salvation for believers. "As you therefore have received Christ Jesus the Lord, so walk in Him, having been firmly rooted and now being built up in Him and established in your faith, just as you were instructed, and overflowing with gratitude."

If your friends accepted the Lord over a period of time while reading through one of the Gospels, then they have been firmly rooted. The next phase of this growth continuum requires regular teaching that will provide more than milk. You have helped lay the foundation in your friends' faith; now you need help in building them up to accept meat as they become established in their faith. Although you want to bring your friends to the point of being able to feed themselves, a good church with regular expository teaching is a necessity to further this process.

2 Timothy 2:15. One of the goals the Lord has given us centers on the priority of Bible study in the Christian's life. Good preaching in a good church should never replace a regular habit of personal Bible study. We should model this truth for our new converts by constantly talking about what we have discovered in our own study. Show your new converts how you study the Scriptures. Give them the tools that you use and help them work through a passage. Get excited about what they're finding in their study. Above all, keep motivating them to make a regular habit of studying the Word, even if it's just fifteen minutes a day. Their lives will be changed more by the habit of Bible study than by the length of time spent on each session.

2 Timothy 3:16–17. Impress on these new believers the process by which the Word works in their lives. God gave every verse to us for our spiritual growth, and that growth takes place through the cycle of four steps found in verse 16. Bible teaching points us in the right direction. Reproof slaps our hand when we stray from the right path. Correction points us back in the right direction. Training in righteousness sets us back on track and carries us farther down that road. The result: a person God can use to do any good work He has planned for that believer to do.

2 Timothy 2:2. Eventually, your new converts will become more mature and should begin to pass on to others what they have learned. The example you gave in reading the Bible with them will guide them more than anything else. Keep reminding them how easy it is just to get together and read the Bible with a friend.

When you start to analyze a church for your friend, *look for the following negative indicators:*

- leaders emphasizing good feelings over expository Bible teaching;
- people sleeping through the sermons, possibly because the preacher does not have the proper spiritual gift for preaching;

- leaders spending more time talking about psychology than the Bible; and
- leaders promoting more experience-oriented groups than Bible studies.

Watch for the following positive things:

- leaders communicating their excitement for the study of the Bible in their own lives;
- systematic expository preaching that predominates over topical preaching;
- adult Sunday school classes offered regularly on books of the Bible, as well as on its study, interpretation, and application; and
- adults leaving the preaching services feeling that God has spoken to them through the Word.

Fellowship

And they were continually devoting themselves to the apostles' teaching and to fellowship, to the breaking of bread and to prayer.

—Acts 2:42

Friendships are always based on things that people have in common. The uniqueness of Christianity brings together people from totally different backgrounds and with completely different interests. They hold Jesus and His Word in common.

Two young married couples once told me that they had absolutely nothing in common except their love for Scripture. One couple enjoyed hunting and fishing; the other couple surrounded themselves with music. As they spent time together, talking about and reading the Bible, they began to grow closer to one another as true friends. Without the common bond of their love for God's Word, they had little reason to continue their friendship.

Leaders in a church with good fellowship will emphasize the Bible as the common ground for believers. Fellowship will be based on Scripture, not on a false definition of "unity" that usually ends up becoming "uniformity," with everyone required to think and act the same way. There can be differences of opinion within biblical unity, but no differences are tolerated within uniformity.

Make a list of all of the passages in the New Testament that contain the words *one another*. This study will spell out the way believers act toward one another in a healthy church with good fellowship.

When you look for a church to attend and support, *note the following negative points:*

- people not fitting in if they don't attend all of the programs;
- leaders pushing programs more than relationships, punctuality emphasized over group interaction and relationships that are rigid, instead of relaxed. Programs do not make people feel welcome; people make people feel welcome;
- newcomers scarcely greeted or welcomed and rarely returning; and
- church discipline swept under the carpet instead of dealt with openly according to Matthew 18; a false view of "love" taught that is concerned with not hurting feelings— so people will stop asking valid questions about what is happening.

Watch for the following positive things:

- leaders who are role models of hospitality and whose homes are open to a lot of people a lot of the time;
- leaders who make themselves accessible to everyone and people who look forward to being visited by them;
- leaders who conduct a strong visitation program to get into the homes of all of the members to shepherd them better; and
- people who are generally friendly to outsiders.

Breaking of Bread

And they were continually devoting themselves to the
apostles' teaching and to fellowship, to the breaking of
bread and to prayer.

—Acts 2:42

When the Lord met with His disciples in the Upper Room in
John 13-14, He instituted the Lord's Supper. He gave His followers a ceremony by which they were to remember Him and
all that He had done and was going to do for them. The Holy
Spirit gave Paul the Apostle more detailed information about
the Lord's Supper in 1 Corinthians 11. You should study this
passage. In Acts 20:7, the believers were coming together regularly every week to remember the Lord's death and His resurrection. This remembrance feast became the central worship meeting
of the local church. Everyone met to remember the Lord.

Some churches equate the breaking of bread with official church
worship and dedicate a separate service to it. The majority of
churches celebrate the Lord's Table at the end of their preaching
service. Still others have exchanged the simplicity of the Last Supper for a complicated, mystical ritual. Although different churches
have different forms of worship, form is never as important as
function and content. You should do a study of the word *worship*
in the Scriptures before deciding on a church. Then you can evaluate worship in light of the Scriptures instead of your emotions or
what makes you feel good in a service. If we have come to worship,
then we have come to remember who Jesus is (His character and
attributes), His past deeds (what He did for us in His death and
resurrection), His current deeds (what He is now doing for us by
making us into His image), and His future deeds (His coming back
to take us home). No matter what form the worship service takes,
it should place Jesus clearly in the center (content) and motivate us
to remember Him (function) as was stated earlier. Singing, praying,
and preaching are all necessary elements of the church, but nothing
should replace Jesus as the center of our worship. Seek out a church
that places a premium on worship, our highest duty to God.

Watch for the following negative things:

- traditions that are more important than worship;
- leaders who consider worship to be just one of the programs of the church, and no one feels that they have missed anything if they don't take part in the worship service;
- the "worship service" doesn't keep Jesus central and doesn't motivate the believers to remember His character and His past, current, and future deeds for us; and
- little or no teaching on 1 Corinthians 11 and on the importance of worship individually and collectively.

Watch for the following positive things:

- leaders give this meeting top priority in their planning of church programs;
- by example, leaders teach members how to worship;
- people are encouraged to come to meet the Lord personally and to praise Him for who He is, what He has done, what He is doing, and what He will do; the Lord—not the preaching, the music, or some performance by a select few believers—is central in this service;
- periodic teaching is given to the church body on the importance and practice of worship.

Prayer

And they were continually devoting themselves to the apostles' teaching and to fellowship, to the breaking of bread and to prayer.

—Acts 2:42

Have you ever heard parents say about their small children, "My children started praying before they were two years old. Isn't it wonderful how they just naturally know how to pray!"

No, you've never heard any parents say that. Children come into this world with a sinful nature that centers life on themselves.

They instinctively know how to eat, sleep, and use up diapers, but the first word that a child learns is usually "Mine!"

Prayer has to be taught. It does not come naturally. In Luke 11, the Lord's disciples asked Him to show them how to pray. They even referred to the fact that John the Baptist had taught his disciples to pray. The Lord answered their request by teaching them the Lord's Prayer. He taught them that prayer requires a selfless, dependent relationship with God. He said nothing about the form of prayer, the location of prayer, the time of day for prayer, or any number of other superfluous items required by various religious groups throughout the centuries. And the Lord continued to teach about prayer by His public and private examples of praying. In John 11, at the grave of Lazarus, He prayed aloud. In John 17, He prayed aloud in private with His disciples.

The Lord speaks to us through our Bible study. We speak with Him through prayer. And the Lord can speak back to us during our times of prayer, although we need to check any "promptings of the Spirit" with Scripture to ensure that it is the Holy Spirit who has spoken and not our own spirit.

When you choose a church for your new believers, look for one that prays individually and collectively. *Watch for the following negative things:*

- church prayers that are lifeless and rote ("And when you are praying, do not use meaningless repetition, as the Gentiles do, for they suppose that they will be heard for their many words" [Matt. 6:7]);
- no teaching on prayer;
- prayer meetings that are gossip sessions, where people pray to impress one another; and
- leaders who use so much theological jargon in their prayers that a new believer would need a college course in "prayer language" to understand them.

Watch for the following positive things:

- leaders and people talking about prayer as part of their everyday life;
- leaders constantly encouraging the people to go to the Lord first with their problems, instead of seeking an answer or solution from other believers;
- leaders teaching on prayer through example by praying publicly in the church and privately with individuals; and
- leaders constantly promoting prayer meetings for the whole church body.

A Perfect Church?

Obviously, you will never find a perfect church. If you ever do find one, please stay away from it unless you are perfect as well.

These guidelines are just that—guidelines. Pray for wisdom from the Lord as you help your new converts find a good church. A bad church can devastate a new believer. New believers are just like new babies. First impressions make a big impact. Make certain that you have taught them to look to the Lord for perfection, not to Christians. We all are hypocrites at times and will remain so until we reach heaven. Prepare these new babies well for the next place in their journey, the church, the most controversial, complex, complicated group of people ever brought together in one building. The Lord died for this group of people, and He is the architect of the church.

"You also, as living stones, are being built up as a spiritual house for a holy priesthood, to offer up spiritual sacrifices acceptable to God through Jesus Christ" (1 Peter 2:5). Be cautious but don't neglect the church.

And when your new believers are integrated into a good church, go find another unsaved person with whom to read the Bible! Do it!

Endnotes

Chapter 1

1. Walter Martin, *Kingdom of the Cults* (Minneapolis, Minn.: Bethany House, 1985), 386-87.

2. Adapted from: James F. Engel and H. Wilbert Norton, *What's Gone Wrong with the Harvest?* (Grand Rapids, Mich.: Zondervan, 1975), 45.

Chapter 2

1. Rebecca M. Pippert, *Out of the Saltshaker: Evangelism as a Way of Life* (Downers Grove, Ill.: InterVarsity, 1979).

2. C. S. Lewis, *The Weight of Glory* (Grand Rapids: Eerdmans, 1949), 15.

Chapter 5

1. James W. Sire, *The Universe Next Door* (Downers Grove, Ill.: InterVarsity, 1988).

2. William Dyrness, *Christian Apologetics in a World Community* (Downers Grove, Ill: InterVarsity, 1983).

Chapter 7

1. F. F. Bruce, *New Testament Documents: Are They Reliable?* (Leicester, England: Inter-Varsity, 1964).

2. Josh McDowell, *Evidence That Demands a Verdict* (San Bernardino, Calif.: Here's Life, 1990).

Chapter 10

1. Walter Martin, *The Kingdom of the Cults* (St. Louis: Bethany, 1985).

Chapter 11

1. F. F. Bruce, *New Testament Documents: Are They Reliable?* (Leicester, England: Inter-Varsity, 1964).

2. Josh McDowell, *Evidence That Demands a Verdict* (San Bernardino, Calif.: Here's Life, 1990).

3. C. S. Lewis, *The Problem of Pain* (repr. ed., New York: Macmillan, 1990).

4. Philip Yancey, *Where Is God When It Hurts?* (Grand Rapids: Zondervan, 1977).